RESIST

35 PROFILES of ORDINARY PEOPLE WHO ROSE UP AGAINST TYRANNY AND INJUSTICE

RESIST

35 PROFILES OF ORDINARY PEOPLE WHO ROSE UP AGAINST TYRANNY AND INJUSTICE

VERONICA CHAMBERS

foreword by

SENATOR CORY BOOKER

HARPER

An Imprint of HarperCollinsPublishers

"When I dare to be powerful, to use my strength
in the service of my vision, then it becomes less and
less important whether I am afraid."
— Audre Lorde

For Flora, Zelah, Sophie, and Alex

Joan of Arc
Martin Luther Chiume
Sojourner Sugiha
Samuel Adams Truth
Ozen the Apache Warrior Schin
Susan B. Anthony Gandhi
ween Liliuokalani Luth
miliano Zapata Ida B. Wells Luth
Lucretia Mott King
Dietrich Bonhoeffer Malcolm
Hedy Lamarr Malcolm X
Dolores Cesar Chavez
Huerta Miriam
nnie Lou Hamer Makeba
Harvey Milk Rachel Carso
angari Maathai Archbishop
Oscar Ro
Malala Yousa

CONTENTS

❧ FOREWORD ❧

NEVER LET YOUR INABILITY TO do everything undermine your determination to do *something*.

The opposite of justice is not injustice; it is inaction, indifference, apathy, and ignorance.

Actions for good, in service of justice—even just one action—standing up against what is wrong, standing up against corrupt power or hate, *will make a difference*.

We are called to use our power to make change. It is why we are here now, because those before us used their power.

This is the story of humanity. It's not the oppressors or oppression that has advanced the world, but those who have stood up against it all—those who have resisted.

There are millions of people and countless more stories from our history that speak to this truth. It is our truth, and it is also our urgent imperative: to pay back the blessings we have inherited from those who have resisted with our own continued struggle, service, and resistance.

May we never be silent in the face of injustice, may we never be still when wrongs persist, and may we always remember our past and those—whose names are often forgotten by history—who stood up for us.

I learned recently about how great resisters changed our reality, my reality.

On March 7, 1965, years before I was born, close to six hundred marchers set out to walk from Selma to Montgomery, Alabama.

The marchers seemingly failed. They ended up bruised and bloody, with bones broken, and on that day would not make it to their final destination.

These Americans were protesting the fact that at that time, black Americans across the country, and particularly in the South, regularly faced harassment, discrimination, and violence from those seeking to prevent them from exercising their constitutional right to vote.

So on that historic day they set out to protest, to walk from Selma to Montgomery.

It was a peaceful protest, a nonviolent demonstration, and yet the marchers were met with violence from Alabama state troopers as they sought to stop and pray on the Edmund Pettus Bridge.

The Alabama state troopers charged into the marchers. They attacked the peaceful protesters with tear gas and billy clubs. The peaceful marchers didn't fight back. Dozens of marchers were severely injured as they were clubbed over their heads and bodies and inhaled the awful chemicals.

That day became known as "Bloody Sunday" because of the injuries sustained by the nonviolent activists, many of whom bled from their wounds from the severe beating.

While these marchers failed to make it to their final destination, their struggle, their willingness to endure such violence, their resistance to oppression, were not in vain.

Because of their courage and the violence they suffered, they succeeded in affecting folks from all over the country who watched what happened to them on television and read about it in newspapers.

One of those people was a man named Arthur Lessman, a young white lawyer living in New Jersey at the time.

When he saw on the news what had happened in Selma, he was horrified. He was sitting comfortably in his home, but the awful scene disturbed his heart and shook his conscience. Something powerful stirred inside him. He knew he couldn't sit by and let this injustice continue—he knew that he must join the fight, join the struggle, and become part of the resistance.

Arthur spoke with his law partner the next day. At first they thought about going to Alabama to join with the nonviolent activists. However, with young families at home and not a lot of money, traveling to Alabama from New Jersey was out of the question.

But Arthur knew he had the power to do *something*, even if it wasn't traveling to the Deep South to march himself. He knew he had to do something to fight against racism and to fight for the rights of black Americans.

Arthur called around to see which people in his area were fighting for racial justice. He couldn't travel to Alabama, but knew that at the very least, he could act right where he was to help the larger cause.

He soon found a group called the Fair Housing Council. This was a group of civil rights activists representing black families who were trying to move into segregated white communities in New Jersey.

Even though at the time it was illegal to discriminate against people when selling a house, it happened all the time across the country and in New Jersey. It was a practice called racial "real estate steering." It meant that realtors would refuse to show a black family houses in predominantly white communities and would steer them only to homes in black communities.

So because of what he saw happening in Selma on TV that day, because of the courage of the marchers in Alabama, because of the inspiration of those who were resisting in another part of the country, Arthur started volunteering with this group dedicated to fighting housing discrimination.

In 1969, years into his work volunteering for racial justice, the Fair Housing Council asked Arthur to help a couple who was looking to buy a home but kept encountering real estate discrimination.

Arthur and the Fair Housing Council helped this couple fight the discrimination they faced and buy the home they loved in a New Jersey town called Harrington Park. With the help of Arthur and the Fair Housing Council, this couple was able to move into a previously segregated neighborhood.

I know this story because that couple was named Cary and Carolyn Booker, and they were my parents.

Because of a young lawyer who was inspired by a group of marchers over one thousand miles away, I got to grow up in my home and my hometown.

This is the power of resistance.

Even if you fail, even if it seems like you may not have made an immediate difference, resistance gives off light amidst darkness, hope amidst despair; it changes hearts and minds even if it doesn't change immediate circumstances.

And in this case, the resistance of marchers on a bridge in Alabama inspired the heart of a lawyer in New Jersey and ultimately changed the outcome of my life before I was even born.

We may never know the full impact of the choices we make and the things we do to stand up for one another and fight for one another. But we must remember that even one action in the cause of justice and righteousness has the power to leap time and space and change the course of history.

That is the story of our history as Americans, of my family and yours, and of so many of our families: people who encountered setbacks and failures, people who experienced pain and suffering, and people who refused to surrender—people who always, always believed that no matter how small it seems, we all have the power and ability to make a difference.

This is the truth you will read about in this incredible book—from Sojourner Truth to Dolores Huerta to Dr. Martin Luther King Jr.—people who stood up and spoke out, not just in big speeches and big gestures, but also in small yet always significant ways. Even when things seemed difficult or impossible, they refused to give in or give up, because they knew they had a special power: to resist injustice and to serve others.

A friend of mine once told me about the stars we see in the sky at night. They are millions of light-years away—so far away that their light takes millions of years to reach us here on Earth, and so far away that in some cases the enormous balls of gas and fire that created the light that we see have already burned out, gone from their constellations in their physical form.

But their light still travels on, and they provide light even on the darkest nights—because energy, warmth, light go on forever, they cannot be destroyed, they are invincible and eternal.

Our lives are illuminated by the lights of our ancestors. You too have a light. You too must decide to let it shine.

The stories in this book are like those stars: they enlighten us, they show us what's possible, and they remind us of our own power to be brilliant.

—Senator Cory Booker

JOAN OF ARC
#resist 1429

"I AM NOT AFRAID. . . . I WAS BORN TO DO THIS."

JOAN OF ARC WAS BORN the daughter of poor farmers in France. At that time, her country was in the middle of what would come to be known as the Hundred Years' War.

Imagine what it was like to live in a country that had been at war for that long. It would mean that the fighting started when you were a little baby and that it would not end until your grandchildren were born, or longer. Nowhere you lived or worked would be safe. Soldiers would fill the streets of your town. There would be no end to the death you witnessed, or to the injuries the people you loved might sustain.

When Joan was thirteen, in the midst of the Hundred Years' War, she began to have visions. In them, she saw herself speaking to the leader of France, Charles, the king's son. She dreamed of riding a horse into battle and helping to end the war.

Joan believed that these waking dreams were divine messages from St. Michael and St. Catherine. She said that the saints told her she would play a role in saving France and urged her to seek an audience with Charles, who had been named dauphin, or heir to the throne.

A lot of people thought Joan was crazy. How could a teenage girl win a battle that grown men had fought and lost for decades?

How could the daughter of poor farmers possibly have advice about how to run the country for the son of the king?

But Joan was resolute—which means she was fiercely determined.

She imagined herself in battle, and she knew she would be victorious. She said, "All battles are first won or lost in the mind."

Joan envisioned her future, then moved forward bravely to turn her dreams into reality. She went to see Robert de Baudricourt, a local leader who supported Charles. At first, he did not know what to make of her: a teenage girl who professed that she must see the man who would be king. But with the village's support, he gave Joan his blessing. She cut her hair short and dressed in men's clothing. On horseback, she made the eleven-day journey across enemy lines to Chinon, where Charles's court resided.

But before Joan was allowed to meet with him, she had to overcome one more obstacle. Charles devised a test: he would dress in common clothes and stand in a crowd of men. If Joan could pick him out of the crowd, he would grant her a meeting.

Joan lived at a time when there was no photography or technology of the kind. And Joan was poor. She had never seen an oil painting. There would have been no way for her to know what Charles VII looked like. Yet she was able to pick him out of the crowd. This led Charles to believe that perhaps there *was* something divine about Joan—and thus perhaps there was a purpose to her mission. She met with Charles and convinced him he needed to take the oath to be king as soon as possible, that the future of France depended on it. She also convinced him to give her a horse and armor and let her ride with the soldiers—all men—into battle.

It was an incredible request, one that no one would reasonably grant. Men fought in wars. Women did not. But Joan resisted the constraints of her time. Charles allowed her to ride into battle.

Joan triumphed in the Siege of Orléans. And when Charles VII was crowned the king of France, she stood by his side.

In 1430, Joan was sent into battle again: this time to Compiègne, where she fought against the Burgundians. There, she was thrown off a horse and captured. Joan was held for several months as her captors tried to sell her off to England. The British thought it might make good propaganda to parade the

teenage "savior of France" into their prisons. Her captors inter-
rogated her, but she never revealed any of France's secrets. They
threatened her, for months on end, with rape and torture. But
again, Joan resisted. She tied her uniform tightly around herself
with dozens of cords. She protected her body and showed them
the force of her will.

Ultimately, it was her gender that her enemies used against
her. They charged her with seventy counts of witchcraft, heresy
(meaning she went against the church), and dressing like a man.
On May 30, 1431, Joan was burned at the stake (a frequent
practice for murdering women who were deemed witches). She
was only nineteen years old.

There is a legend that says although Joan's body was burned
that day, when the fires died down, her heart was discovered
unburned and intact: a symbol that she was pure of heart.

The Hundred Years' War continued for more than twenty
years, but the efforts Joan made to shore up the reign of Charles
VII had been profound, and his position as king was never in
danger again. In 1456, he declared Joan innocent of all charges
and she was named a martyr.

Joan would go on to be called a saint by the Catholic
Church. Throughout the world, she is a symbol of how much
good one person can do when she listens to her heart and gives
of herself selflessly.

It is hard to believe that some people still use the phrase
"just a girl." By that, they mean that young women could not

possibly have real power. Because of Joan of Arc, we know better. Yes, she was just a girl. But she was also "just" the most amazing warrior of her time.

#RESIST LESSON

ASK YOURSELF: WHAT WAS I BORN TO DO?

MARTIN LUTHER
#resist 1517

"WHATEVER YOUR HEART CLINGS TO AND CONFIDES IN, THAT IS REALLY YOUR GOD."

MARTIN LUTHER'S FATHER WANTED HIM to be a lawyer. At first, Martin obeyed. He dutifully attended school in Germany in pursuit of a law degree. But one afternoon, after visiting his parents, as he was riding back to the university on horseback, he was caught in a terrible thunderstorm.

He prayed, making a promise to the saints that if his life was spared, he would become a monk. After the storm subsided and he was safe, he went home to tell his parents about his promise. They reluctantly accepted his decision. (Some say the truth was that Martin wanted to become a monk all along. The thunderstorm was just a clever way to get his father off his back.)

Either way, from that moment on, Martin Luther learned

how to forge his own path rather than blindly follow what others pushed him to do.

He was also learning how to listen to his own heart, which is not always easy.

Because although he became a monk, he did not feel comfortable with some of the rules and regulations of the Catholic Church.

The prayers were in Latin—which most people did not understand.

Churchgoers were also told that they were not worthy of speaking directly to God, that they needed to take their prayers—their hopes, their dreams, their confessions—to priests, who would take their messages to God for them.

The church also allowed people to buy forgiveness for the things they did wrong, by purchasing something called an "indulgence."

An indulgence was a payment that you could make to the church to forgive your sins. Indulgences allowed the church to get richer. The idea that people with money could be forgiven more easily than the poor did not sit right with Martin.

Martin believed that all people were equal in the eyes of God. He thought that the ministers of the church should not stand between the common people and their god.

He dreamed of a simpler way—a church where people could pray in their own language, where men and women could take their prayers directly to their god. He believed forgiveness should be not bought, but earned.

In those days, church doors were like community billboards: it was where people went to read the news. Martin wrote his criticisms of the Catholic Church—ninety-five of them!—onto a piece of paper and nailed it to the church door.

It might all have ended there, a few people walking in and out of the church and glancing at Martin Luther's words on their way to work and school.

But Martin's declarations were posted at a time when the printing press was growing in popularity. That simple piece of technology meant that many, many copies of Martin's message could be made. And they were!

Within two weeks, Martin's words were read in every city and every town in Germany.

Within two months, his words had been read throughout Europe.

He was called a heretic by the Catholic Church and excommunicated, which means "thrown out." He left and began a new faith, which is now known as Protestantism. (The word "protest" is, appropriately, built right in there.)

Martin Luther has come to symbolize the notion of freedom of religion—meaning that we should all get to choose if, when, and how we pray.

At the time, the Catholic Church was one of the most powerful institutions in the world. The image of Martin nailing his criticisms to the church door is synonymous with the courage it takes to stand up to any power larger than you.

When a person chooses to resist, they rarely know how many people will stand with them. It may be hundreds. It may be millions. It may not, at first, be very many at all.

But what we learn from the life of Martin Luther is that one person can change what was previously thought to be impossible. But before that can happen, we must dare to be the first to stand.

#RESIST LESSON

ONE VOICE CAN SHAKE THE EARTH.

GALILEO GALILEI
#resist 1609

🌿

"WE CANNOT TEACH PEOPLE ANYTHING. WE CAN ONLY HELP THEM DISCOVER IT WITHIN THEMSELVES."

WHEN GALILEO WAS SEVENTEEN YEARS old, he looked up at a chandelier swinging from a fixture in the ceiling and watched it go back and forth. Sometimes the movement was big, like when you're on a swing in the playground and you push off hard and go sailing into the sky. Sometimes the movement was soft, just a gentle swaying back and forth like grass in the wind. What he noticed was that no matter whether the swing was big or small, it had the same pace. It seemed to match the rhythm of his heartbeat. A hundred years later, a Dutch scientist named Christiaan Huygens would use the same observations to make the world's first clock. In this and so many ways, Galileo was far ahead of his time.

There are people who can see only what's in front of them: a lamp or an apple, a sunrise or a sunset. Then there are people who see what's in front of them and ask *why?* and *why not?* We have a lot of names for people who ask great questions. We call those people scientists and inventors, philosophers and astronomers. Galileo was all of those things. He was a man who asked beautiful questions.

When he first heard about the invention of the telescope in Holland, he sat in his studio in Italy and made a better, more sophisticated, more powerful version—without any written plans or guidance.

He used that telescope to look deep into the night sky, and there he discovered things no one else had yet seen: the mountains and valleys on the surface of the moon, Saturn's rings, sunspots, the four largest moons of the planet Jupiter, and the phases of the planet Venus.

Galileo published his findings in a pamphlet he called *Sidereus Nuncius,* or *Starry Messenger.*

For his discoveries, he was appointed primary mathematician at the court of his patron, the Grand Duke of Tuscany. But all his questioning eventually got him into hot water.

Most of the world's scientists at the time believed that the Earth was the center of the universe. The Catholic Church endorsed this belief. God, they believed, surely would have put humans, his creation, at the center of everything.

But because of his keen observations, Galileo believed that the sun was the center of our solar system and that the Earth circled the sun once a year. That's called "heliocentrism," and Galileo was right about it.

Heliocentrism doesn't seem like such a big deal now. But it is as true today as it was in the age of Galileo: when you disagree with a majority of people, when you question the teaching of powerful institutions, you risk getting into seriously deep trouble.

The Catholic Church had begun the Inquisition, a period of great oppression. Anyone who disagreed with the church's opinion risked conviction, imprisonment, torture, and even death. The church accused Galileo of heresy, but Galileo prized truth above his own freedom, so he kept telling it. And because he told the truth about what he saw, future scientists were able to build on his knowledge. His motion experiments would later inspire Isaac Newton's work with gravity. Galileo's inventions—his compasses and balances and the way that he refined early crude versions of telescopes and microscopes—became invaluable to future biologists and astronomers. Even the techniques he used to conduct his experiments laid the groundwork for the modern scientific age.

It seems so simple: look up at the sky, write down what you see, tell everyone about it. But that is what revolutionaries do: they make us see the truth of the world, even when it runs counter to everything we've been taught before. Through that truth, we, and the world, are changed.

#RESIST LESSON

ASK QUESTIONS. THERE IS NO END TO WHAT IS WAITING TO BE DISCOVERED.

SAMUEL ADAMS

#resist 1773

"'JUST AND TRUE LIBERTY, EQUAL AND IMPARTIAL LIBERTY' . . . IS A THING THAT ALL MEN ARE CLEARLY ENTITLED TO."

SOME PEOPLE KNOW, FROM A very early age, exactly what they want to do with their lives. Samuel Adams was not one of those people.

He tried and failed to run a brewing company. He tried and failed to be a newspaper publisher.

By many measures, Samuel Adams was . . . a failure. But failure isn't fatal. Failure means that you *tried*. And many times, the skills you learn from *trying* come in handy much later and in unexpected ways. Sam found this out at the dawn of a new nation.

Sam lived in Boston when Massachusetts was only a colony

and the British ruled over each of the thirteen colonies in the west.

Samuel Adams's moment came in 1764. The British government had won the French and Indian War. But wars are expensive, and the government was deep in debt. England began taxing the American colonies as a way to refill its coffers after the war.

First came the Sugar Act. The British placed a steep tax on sugar, an item they knew that every colonial household used every day.

Samuel stepped forward and made an impassioned speech against what would eventually be referred to as "taxation without representation."

That meant British citizens living in the colonies were entitled to their own governing bodies, but they were *not* offered a chance to be a part of the British Parliament—where the taxes went and where it was decided how they should be spent. It was wrong, Sam declared at a Boston town meeting, for the colonies to be subject to a tax they hadn't been allowed to vote on and weren't allowed to benefit from.

Samuel wrote a list of instructions for the Massachusetts House of Representatives to act upon, rejecting the Sugar Act.

This was a bold step. Samuel's leadership led Massachusetts to become the first colony to speak up against unjust British taxes.

Samuel was also the first leader on record to state that the colonies should unite in their opposition to the British.

Until that point, the colonies had operated separately, each making its own rules for its residents. But Samuel knew they were stronger together than they could ever be apart.

The next year, the British passed the Stamp Act, which placed a steep tax on all printed material. Again, Samuel wrote the instructions on how the Massachusetts House of Representatives should respond.

Because he was a powerful writer, because he took the time to think through his ideas, commit them to paper, and share them with those in charge, Samuel helped to spark the notion that the colonists need not obey British rule. They were citizens, after all. They had rights.

When the British placed a steep tax on tea, Samuel helped to orchestrate the famous Boston Tea Party, a political protest in which demonstrators, some in disguise, boarded the British ships and threw chests of tea into Boston Harbor.

The British were furious, but the seeds of revolution were beginning to take root. The colonies would no longer tolerate being ruled from afar and used to fill purses in London. They would have their own government. They would have their independence.

In 1774, leaders of the colonies gathered for the First Continental Congress in Philadelphia. Samuel Adams was there.

The famous colonial figure Paul Revere was there too. Revere was a talented silversmith and an engraver. He drew a portrait of Sam in Philadelphia that today hangs in the Yale University Art Gallery.

George Washington, who would become the first president of the United States of America, was also in attendance.

By the Second Continental Congress, their ranks had grown to include more than three hundred men, including Alexander Hamilton, who would serve at George Washington's side in the American Revolution and go on to design the new nation's financial system. Also in attendance was Hamilton's longtime foe Thomas Jefferson, who would be the principal author of the Declaration of Independence and the third president of the United States.

Sam was ambitious for the nation, but not for himself. He purposely did not seek out fame. Yet when the Revolutionary War began in Boston and British soldiers fought against the American troops at the Battles of Lexington and Concord, the British soldiers had among their aims the arrest of John Hancock . . . and Samuel Adams. The British knew how important Sam's writing and leadership were. Paul Revere, the engraver who drew Sam's portrait at the First Continental Congress, saved Sam's life that night. Revere's midnight ride on horseback through the streets of Boston, in which he famously called out, "The British are coming! The British are coming!" allowed Sam and John Hancock to escape.

There are some people who change history by being the heroes we read about: they charge into war, they overthrow their enemies, they become presidents and kings. Their glory shines around them.

Others fight not for personal glory, but for the glory of a nation.

Samuel Adams was the man behind the scenes. He had the diligence to organize committees, the vision to make plans, and the self-confidence to carry those plans through.

Sam set fires but also had the patience to strategize at a time when hotter heads might have prevailed. He had the discipline to work the many long hours it took to build both a revolution and a new nation.

Sam eventually became governor of Massachusetts. He helped his cousin John Adams become the second president of the United States. John said that Samuel's work created and "tempered a wedge of steel to split the knot . . . that tied America to Britain." Without the work of men like Samuel Adams, revolution is impossible.

#RESIST LESSON

THE STEADINESS OF COMMITMENT CAN DO MORE IN THE LONG TERM THAN UNSUSTAINABLE SPARKS.

FREDERICK DOUGLASS

#resist 1841

"IF THERE IS NO STRUGGLE, THERE IS NO PROGRESS."

IT IS ONE OF THE most difficult contradictions to bear in American history. From 1775 to 1783, colonists fought against the British for American independence. After the war, most Northern states moved to abolish the slave trade—the legalized institution of owning another human being as property. But because of the boom in the cotton industry in the South, Southern plantation owners, who depended on slave labor to keep their profit margins high, fought—successfully—to preserve the practice.

Enslaved people did backbreaking work in the fields for no pay. Fear was a large part of how slave owners and their employees, called overseers, kept the system of slavery going. Common punishments included whipping, beating, branding with a hot iron, shackling and imprisonment, and hanging. Many people in the North had no idea of the depth of the abuse in slavery. It was considered a scandal when one New York man in the 1800s reported that "at least three-quarters of the male slaves he saw at sale had scars on their backs from whipping."

In order to further discourage enslaved people from resisting or plotting escape, they were forbidden to learn how to read or write. Families were broken apart and sold to different plantations, all with the aim of keeping the enslaved isolated, broken in spirit, alone, and helpless.

Frederick Douglass was born on a plantation where he was exposed to the worst of slavery. Violent whippings were common. Although the enslaved spent hours in the field, they were underfed and spent many a night cold and hungry.

When Frederick was seven, his mother died.

When he was eight, he was sent to live with a ship's carpenter named Hugh Auld.

There he secretly learned to read and write. He learned about abolitionists, the movement by people—both black and white—working to end slavery. He was still enslaved, but he spent seven years in peace. There were no whippings. He had food and a warm bed to sleep in at night.

At fifteen, his fortunes changed. He was sold off to a slave owner named Edward Covey.

Covey was so brutal that he had gained the reputation of

being a "slave breaker." He used every tactic; he did not just whip his slaves to the point where they were more dead than alive, he broke their spirits, and bodies mend more easily than souls.

Frederick Douglass suffered all that and more. Finally, he said, "Enough." He vowed that within a year, he would escape and no longer live as a slave.

On his first attempt, he was found out and thrown in jail.

He tried to escape a second time and was jailed again.

There is a saying that exemplifies the kind of hope Frederick clung to in that jail cell: A delay is not a denial.

Frederick had been thwarted, but he did not give up.

He worked at a shipyard for two years until he could accomplish his dream. On September 3, 1838, he escaped Baltimore, and in twenty-four hours he was in New York City. He lived the rest of his days as a free man.

Frederick Douglass said, "I prayed for twenty years but received no answer until I prayed with my legs."

Frederick kept reading, determined in freedom to continue the education that had been denied him as a slave. He subscribed to William Lloyd Garrison's weekly journal, the *Liberator*. In 1841, he went to see Garrison speak at the Bristol County Anti-Slavery Society's annual meeting in New Bedford, Massachusetts.

Garrison's speech inspired Frederick in a way that changed both their lives. It's a good idea to be on the lookout for speeches like that. Hearing great thinkers speak, whether in person or online, can set you off in a new direction. Great speeches give us hope when we are weary. They give us new ideas when we feel stuck and uninspired. They remind us that the word "impossible" contains hidden within it the most important idea—"possible."

After Garrison's speech, Frederick wrote, "No face and form ever impressed me with such sentiments [the hatred of slavery] as did those of William Lloyd Garrison."

Inspired by Garrison, Frederick decided to take to the stage and tell *his* story. He was just twenty-three years old when he gave his first speech at the Massachusetts Anti-Slavery Society's annual convention in Nantucket.

William Lloyd Garrison was so impressed that he agreed to mentor Frederick and invited him to become a lecturer for the society for the next three years.

By escaping slavery, by telling his story, Frederick Douglass did not change just his own life. He began to change the world he had been born into.

In 1845, Frederick published his autobiography *Narrative of the Life of Frederick Douglass, an American Slave, Written by Himself.*

It was a brave act, because the information in the autobiography could endanger his freedom. It was not unusual for bounty hunters to try to recapture slaves who had escaped and throw them back into slavery.

But Frederick knew that slavery's greatest protection was that the details of its operation were kept secret from many

Americans outside of the South.

He had seen it every time he gave a speech. When he told white Americans who had never seen slavery up close just how brutal and dehumanizing the practice was, they were ignited and determined to bring an end to slavery. The more good people knew about how plantations were run and how men, women, and children were treated, the more the tide turned.

Frederick was frightened, but he published his autobiography to international acclaim. He traveled to England, Ireland, and Scotland, sharing his message. He met with President Abraham Lincoln during the Civil War, and he recruited black soldiers for the Union army.

The more he spoke, the more people joined him in his quest. Slavery had to end. Enough was, truly, enough.

#RESIST LESSON

IT IS JUST ONE WORD, BUT THESE SIX LETTERS ARE ENOUGH TO START A REVOLUTION: ENOUGH.

SOJOURNER TRUTH
#resist 1850

"I FEEL SAFE IN THE MIDST OF MY ENEMIES, FOR THE TRUTH IS ALL POWERFUL AND WILL PREVAIL."

AS A LITTLE GIRL, SHE thought she had nothing.

She had been born into slavery, an institution that had taught her that she *was* nothing.

When Sojourner Truth was nine years old, she was sold from one plantation to another. The price for her life was $100 and a gaggle of sheep. She never saw her mother again.

She did not think she was powerful. A little girl, born enslaved, in a time when human beings could be traded like farm animals. But she was wrong.

When she was twenty-nine, she escaped slavery. Eventually, she met two men who would change her life. One of the men was white. His name was William Lloyd Garrison. The other man was black. His name was Frederick Douglass. They were abolitionists, which meant they worked to put an end to slavery.

Garrison and Douglass believed that Sojourner had a story to tell. She could not read or write. It was forbidden for slaves to learn how to do either. But she had her voice, and the men encouraged her to use it.

Sojourner began to give lectures, and wherever she went, people gathered to hear her speak. She stood six feet tall, and because she'd been raised on a plantation owned by a Dutch family, she spoke English with a soft Dutch accent. Harriet Beecher Stowe, who would go on to write one of the most scathing indictments of slavery, *Uncle Tom's Cabin,* found Sojourner mesmerizing. Stowe said she had never "been conversant with anyone who had more of that silent and subtle power which we call personal presence than this woman."

It's a good reminder: Not all powerful people shout. On the contrary, it's been said that real power whispers.

Sojourner met the leaders of the women's movement, Elizabeth Cady Stanton and Susan B. Anthony, and they encouraged her to speak out not just against slavery, but also for women's rights. Sojourner began to speak about the importance of not separating one from the other. She said:

"There is a great stir about colored men getting their rights, but not a word about colored women; and if colored men get their rights and not colored women theirs, you see the colored men will be masters over the women and it will be just as bad as it was before. So I am for keeping the thing going while things are stirring; because if we wait till it is still, it will take a great while to get it going again."

Her words were prophetic. Freed black men were granted the right to vote in 1870 by the Fifteenth Amendment to the Constitution. Women would not be granted the right to vote for another fifty years: in 1920, by the Nineteenth Amendment to the Constitution.

Sojourner learned that she had more truths to tell than she could imagine. One of her speeches, "Ain't I a Woman?," is still regarded as one of the greatest ever given.

She was born a slave. She was born a woman.

They told her she was nothing.

But she did have something.

She had her voice.

#RESIST LESSON

WE ALL HAVE THE POWER TO SPEAK UP AND SPEAK OUT.

SUSAN B. ANTHONY
#resist 1853

"FORGET CONVENTIONALISMS; FORGET WHAT THE WORLD WILL SAY, WHETHER YOU ARE IN YOUR PLACE OR OUT OF YOUR PLACE; THINK YOUR BEST THOUGHTS, SPEAK YOUR BEST WORDS, DO YOUR BEST WORKS, LOOKING TO YOUR OWN CONSCIENCE FOR APPROVAL."

HER FATHER TAUGHT HER A lesson she would never forget: You must do right even when the people around you dare to say it is wrong.

It was a time when women's education wasn't valued. But her father sent her to school anyway.

Slavery was legal and many whites did not speak up against it. Her father spoke up against slavery anyway.

Susan learned directly from her father the importance of

choosing what is right over what is easy.

When her family moved to Rochester, New York, they all became involved in the antislavery movement. Her brothers, Daniel and Merritt, moved to Kansas and were active abolitionists there. Susan joined the American Anti-Slavery Society. She took on every task, from making speeches to putting up posters and passing out leaflets.

This was brave work for a woman to do. Some days, slavery supporters threw objects at her. Those were the easy days. Susan received death threats and was confronted by mobs of angry slavery supporters. They made an effigy, or a life-size doll, that was meant to represent Susan and they dragged the effigy through the streets by a rope.

It was terrifying to be confronted by the force of so much hate. But Susan never cowered. She kept going. She resisted.

When the Thirteenth Amendment was passed and slavery was abolished, Susan hoped that the Republican Party would thank women like her for their support and make it legal for women to vote.

But the men in charge saw things differently. They saw the rights of slaves and the rights of women as entirely different matters.

Susan was more than disappointed. She felt betrayed. But she had made a promise to herself a long time before. She was dedicated to equal rights for *all* people, for *both* genders. She would keep going.

Susan was strengthened in her resolve to get women the vote by her friendship with Elizabeth Cady Stanton.

Having a friend who shared the same vision, who was equally dedicated to the work, made the struggle a little easier to bear.

Together, Elizabeth and Susan founded the American Equal Rights Association. They also started a newspaper called *The Revolution.* The motto at the top of the newspaper's masthead read:

"PRINCIPLE, NOT POLICY: JUSTICE, NOT FAVORS.—MEN, THEIR RIGHTS AND NOTHING MORE: WOMEN, THEIR RIGHTS AND NOTHING LESS."

The newspaper promised to work on behalf of "justice for all."

Susan left no one out in her fight for equality. She began to work as a labor activist and was one of the early proponents of the eight-hour workday and equal pay for equal work. At the time, it was common for factory workers to work twelve-hour days. In factories, women were always paid less than men.

Educational equality was another of Susan's passions. She had been a teacher for years early in her career and never forgot the impact a teacher can have on the life of a child—the value of a teacher's work in society. As part of her work with the American Equal Rights Association, she argued for better pay for women teachers (who were also paid less than their male counterparts).

At the New York State Teachers Association convention, Susan campaigned for coeducation, which meant boys and girls attending school together—something unheard of at the time. Her argument: There were no differences between the minds of men and women.

In the 1890s, the University of Rochester was persuaded to allow its first class of women to study there. Susan was challenged with the task of raising $50,000 to support their tuition. Women attending university was an incredible achievement. Susan eagerly took on the task. When the pledges came in short and she was up against the deadline, Susan offered the cash value of her own life insurance policy to the university. Equality for all. Justice for all. She was willing to stake her life on it.

But gaining the right for women to vote was her driving force. Some states gave the right to women early. Wyoming Territory, for example, gave women the vote in 1869.

But for Susan, state law was too tenuous, too malleable, for something as important as the right to vote. She wanted a constitutional amendment, a law that would last for generations to come.

She kept returning to Congress every year from 1869 to 1906, the year that she died. In 1877, when she gathered ten thousand signatures in a petition, she took them to Congress.

The men in office laughed at her. She never gave up. She believed with every fiber of her being that the suffrage amendment, the right for women to vote, would pass.

Her energy surprised the men in Congress, some of whom were half her age. She said, "The older I get, the greater power I seem to have to help the world; I am like a snowball—the further I am rolled the more I gain."

Susan did not live to see women get the right to vote. It came almost a decade and a half after her death. But her stamp on the effort was so well recognized that the Nineteenth Amendment, which expands the Constitution to give women the right to vote, is also known as "the Susan B. Anthony amendment."

#RESIST LESSON

SISTERHOOD CAN FUEL A REVOLUTION.

LOZEN THE APACHE WARRIOR

#resist 1860

"STRONG AS A MAN, BRAVER THAN MOST, AND CUNNING IN STRATEGY, LOZEN IS A SHIELD TO HER PEOPLE."

—Victorio, Lozen's brother

WE LEARN WHAT IS POSSIBLE from what we've seen or been taught. It happens all the time: people make assumptions based upon what they've experienced in the past. When Lozen was a girl, no one had ever seen an Apache woman warrior. The women in her tribe expected her to behave in the same way the other girls did. She would cook, they thought, and take care of the children, and stay at home.

Lozen wanted something different. She wanted to learn

how to ride horses, shoot bows and arrows, be a warrior.

She asked her brother, Victorio, to teach her. And he did. She became a great equestrian, riding horses with speed and dexterity.

Lozen was a natural at archery. With her bow and arrow, she could hit every shot.

She earned the name Lozen, "Horse Stealer," after she successfully robbed horses from her enemies in a raid.

She could fight in battle as well as any man.

But she also learned the Native American art of making natural medicines.

She became someone who could heal as well as a soldier who might wound.

During this time, white American settlers were expanding their territory. They were using military troops to force the Native American tribes from their land.

Lozen wanted her people, the Apache, to keep what had been theirs for generations. Lozen and Victorio fought against those who wanted to push the Apache off their land and move them to prison-like reservations.

The American quest to take the Native Americans' land was relentless. In 1870, Lozen and her people were forced onto the land that, years later, officially became the San Carlos Reservation in Arizona. Seven years after that, they fought their way back to their homeland.

They were sent, two years later, to another reservation.

They kept fighting.

In 1880, Lozen's beloved brother was killed in battle. Lozen took a group of warriors and sought revenge, raiding American settlements in New Mexico and Arizona.

She joined forces with the great Apache chief Geronimo. But even he could not keep the Americans at bay forever. He surrendered in 1886. Lozen and her tribe were captured and sent to Florida, then Alabama. Not used to those warm climates, many of them perished of disease.

The men and women in her tribe had never seen a young woman like Lozen. By becoming the type of person she dreamed of, she redefined for girls everywhere what was possible.

#RESIST LESSON

YOUR MOST POWERFUL WEAPON IS YOUR MIND.

SITTING BULL

#resist 1865

"I HAVE SEEN NOTHING THAT THE WHITE MAN HAS, HOUSES OR RAILWAYS OR CLOTHING OR FOOD, THAT IS AS GOOD AS THE RIGHT TO MOVE IN OPEN COUNTRY AND LIVE IN OUR OWN FASHION."

HE WAS BORN IN THE Great Plains of America, to one of the seven Lakota tribes. These tribes held more than half a million miles of territory. They traveled with the buffalo across a great green expanse that includes the land we now call Montana, Nebraska, North Dakota, South Dakota, and Wyoming.

When he was born, his father called him Jumping Badger. It turned out that was mainly wishful thinking. The people in his tribe called him by another nickname. They called him

Slow because he was *not* the type to jump forward. He moved so slowly, it was as if you could see him thinking through every step.

Sometimes it's good to go slow.

When he was ten years old, he killed his first buffalo. This was an important rite of passage in the Lakota tradition. The buffalo would feed the tribe for many days. But while he was proud of this accomplishment, he also felt the pain of causing death. He knelt down next to the buffalo and whispered, "Thank you, Brother Buffalo, for giving your life so that my people will live."

We tend to think of great warriors as those who fight. But Sitting Bull became a legend because of the way he did *not* move in battle.

It takes a lot of courage to sit still when the enemy is coming at you. When someone is attacking you with their words, or something even worse, it is very, very difficult to stay calm. But there is a part of fighting back that takes place in your mind. It is hard to find wisdom when you're reacting quickly and emotionally. You might make a better choice if you can pause for even a moment or two.

The Lakota people were embroiled in a great battle to protect their land. At first, when the white settlers came, they seemed to want to merely trade with the Indian people. The Lakota exchanged their furs and warm buffalo skins for the items the white men had: horses, guns, wagons, coffee, kettles, and sugar.

But then the white men came back in larger numbers. They built army forts and manned them with many soldiers. Then the soldiers began to drive the native tribes from their land. Sitting Bull believed that land was life. He was prepared to share the land with the white settlers, but he was determined that his people not be driven from their homes.

In one of Sitting Bull's most famous battles, he led four warriors out into enemy lines, near the Yellowstone River. The five men sat and smoked a pipe as bullets whizzed past them. The American soldiers watched, confused, as Sitting Bull finished his pipe, cleaned it out, and calmly walked away.

Matters escalated in 1874, when General George Armstrong Custer confirmed that gold had been found in the Black Hills of the Lakota territory.

The greed for land was now overshadowed by the lust for gold.

The Black Hills were a sacred land to many tribes and had been protected from white settlement by the Fort Laramie Treaty of 1868. But prospectors ignored the treaty, and the government pushed Sitting Bull's tribe to sell.

When he refused to sell the land, the government declared that any Lakota who had not moved to a reservation by January 31, 1876, would be considered hostile. Sitting Bull held fast.

The freedom that he had known as a child was what he fought for. He wanted his children, and their children's children, to know what it was like to roam the Great Plains as his people had done for generations. He said, "When I was a boy, the Sioux owned the world. The sun rose and set on their land. They sent ten thousand men to battle. Where are the warriors today? Who slew them? Where are our lands? Who owns them?"

As the American troops advanced toward his people, Sitting Bull called for a meeting at Rosebud Creek in the Montana Territory. He invited the Lakota, the Cheyenne, and the Arapaho tribes. He led them in a sun dance and offered prayers to the Great Spirit, Wakan Tanka. He had a vision that day: of the American soldiers falling like grasshoppers out of the sky. He thought the vision was a good omen; perhaps victory was within their grasp.

Crazy Horse, the Oglala Lakota war chief, advanced first with five hundred warriors in his band. He surprised the Americans and forced them to retreat at the Battle of the Rosebud. Three thousand more warriors joined them at the Little Bighorn River, and on June 25, Sitting Bull and his warriors defeated General Custer's troops. He pushed the American troops to a ridge where they fell over in defeat, just as he had seen in his vision.

Any soldier knows that there are few things more valuable in battle than the element of surprise.

Sometimes that calm, that stillness, is the thing they never see coming.

#RESIST LESSON

THE FIRST STEP IS TO STAND YOUR GROUND.

QUEEN LILIUOKALANI

#resist 1881

"THE WAY TO LOSE ANY EARTHLY KINGDOM IS TO BE INFLEXIBLE, INTOLERANT AND PREJUDICIAL. ANOTHER WAY IS TO BE TOO FLEXIBLE, TOLERANT OF TOO MANY WRONGS AND WITHOUT JUDGMENT AT ALL. IT IS A RAZOR'S EDGE. IT IS THE WIDTH OF A BLADE OF PILI GRASS."

AS A LITTLE GIRL, SHE loved growing up in Hawaii. Her country was one nation made of hundreds of little islands and eight big ones, spread across the Pacific Ocean. The big islands were Niʻihau, Kauaʻi, Oʻahu, Molokaʻi, Lānaʻi, Kahoʻolawe, Maui, and the island of Hawaiʻi. She loved how the tropical breezes blew warm across her skin and how the ocean shone blue in every direction. When she looked up at the mountains and volcanoes, she felt that she might live a hundred lifetimes and never climb every rocky crevice. Hawaii was vast and majestic, a paradise, and one day she would be its queen.

Lili loved music and dedicated herself to learning both traditional European and classic Hawaiian instruments. She played the guitar, the piano, the ukulele, and the zither. She learned to sing in Hawaiian and English. She wrote and published more than 160 songs.

Music kept her company when she was lonely. Music made her feel strong when she felt weak. She wrote, "To compose was as natural to me as to breathe; and this gift of nature, never having been suffered to fall into disuse, remains a source of the greatest consolation to this day. . . . Hours of which . . . I might have found long and lonely, passed quickly and cheerfully by, occupied and soothed by the expression of my thoughts in music."

Years later, Liliuokalani's brother was king and left on a royal trip around the world. He appointed her the temporary sovereign of Hawaii, the ruler, while he was away.

During her brother's absence, disease broke out. This time, the medical crisis was a smallpox epidemic and many Hawaiians perished. Liliuokalani lost her sister and several of her closest friends. The way that the disease was ravaging the community felt frightening and familiar. She was the interim queen and decided to close the borders of the island until the disease was under control.

Sugar was the greatest export in Hawaii at the time. The wealthy sugar growers were furious at the temporary queen, because every day the ports were closed, they were losing money. But Lili resisted. She knew that every day the ports were closed, the people of Hawaii were saving lives.

The smallpox conflict pointed to struggles that were to come. The white American businessmen who were making huge profits in Hawaii did not want a native woman like Liliuokalani in charge.

The United States had been looking to expand its power in the early 1800s. The men who had fought so valiantly against the British also admired the reach and scope of the British Empire. But by this time, there were very few lands left to conquer. Noncolonized countries were few and far away. The Founding Fathers of the United States worried that they did not have the might to conquer countries in Africa or Asia. Some islands in the Pacific were of interest, however. The Hawaiian Islands, located strategically between Asia and the United States, were among them.

American Christian missionaries began to arrive in Hawaii in the 1820s. These men and women did vital volunteer work, but they were also on a recruiting mission to get native Hawaiians to join their churches. By the 1840s, the leaders of Hawaii began to fear the impact of foreign countries such as the United

States. They knew that Hawaii's lush landscape, so rich with agricultural bounty, would be very attractive to those whose focus was on financial gain.

When Liliuokalani succeeded her brother and became queen, the US Congress enacted the McKinley Tariff, a bill designed to protect certain American businesses from foreign competition. This put an enormous tax on all sugar exported from Hawaii to the United States. Similar to the Sugar Act and Tea Act taxes that the British had imposed on the colonies, the McKinley Tariff made the Americans richer and the Hawaiians poorer in the process.

The white businessmen in Hawaii began to consolidate their power. They formed a militia called the Honolulu Rifles. This volunteer military group consisted solely of white Hawaiian residents. Then in 1887, they penned the Constitution of the Kingdom of Hawaii. This limited voting rights for the governing House of Nobles to men of a prescribed income level and of white, European, and Hawaiian backgrounds. Because of the required income levels, the House of Nobles quickly became a group of powerful, rich men, most of whom were white Americans and Europeans.

These men claimed to support American democratic ideals, but they were against Queen Liliuokalani. She was a woman, and they believed the power should be with men. She was a native Hawaiian, with tan skin. They believed that Hawaii should be ruled by white Americans.

Queen Liliuokalani fought back, and the businessmen in Hawaii made a secret plot against her. Under the false pretense that the rebellion threatened American businesses, the US Marines attacked Hawaii, and the American flag was raised above the palace, symbolizing that Hawaii had been conquered.

Liliuokalani was forced to abdicate her throne, and Sanford B. Dole was appointed the first president of the Republic of Hawaii. Liliuokalani believed that he did not love the people the way she did. She feared that men like Dole were interested solely in the profits they could reap from Hawaii's rich natural resources. In 1895, she led a rebellion that was unsuccessful.

As her final act of resistance, Liliuokalani wrote a song about her sadness for the nation that she loved. The song was called "Aloha Oe," which means "Farewell to Thee." "Aloha Oe" is one of the most beloved songs in Hawaiian history, and many consider it to be the island's unofficial anthem.

In 1898 Hawaii was annexed, and in 1959 it became America's fiftieth state.

Liliuokalani was the last queen of Hawaii, forever beloved for her bravery in choosing human life and defending the rich culture of her people over monetary wealth.

Her life reminds us that even when we do not succeed in our goals, there is a tremendous value in clarifying and acting upon our ideas. As Liliuokalani once wrote to her daughter, "I could not turn back the time for political change but there is still time to save our heritage. You must remember never to cease to act because you fear you may fail."

#RESIST LESSON

DO NOT LET FEAR OF FAILURE PREVENT YOU FROM TRYING.

LUCRETIA MOTT
#resist 1883

"ANY GREAT CHANGE MUST EXPECT OPPOSITION BECAUSE IT SHAKES THE VERY FOUNDATION OF PRIVILEGE."

SHE WAS JUST AN ORDINARY girl who loved to read. Her father was a Nantucket sea captain. She loved their life by the shore. Then one day, she picked up a book called *Mental Improvement: Or the Beauties and Wonders of Nature and Art in a Series of Instructive Conversations* by a woman named Priscilla Wakefield. The book had a lot of valuable lessons about life by the sea: whaling and seashells, stained glass and the art of navigation. The book also talked about slavery—how violent it was, how inhumane the practice could be. It wasn't what she expected when she picked up the book, but once she finished reading, Lucretia Mott was never the same.

She moved south and cofounded the Philadelphia Female Anti-Slavery Society. Her husband, James, supported her in her quest for equal rights. Together, they made their Philadelphia home a stop on the Underground Railroad, a secret alliance of citizens who worked together to help enslaved people escape from the South to the North.

She traveled to London to speak at the World Anti-Slavery Convention. But the convention leaders, all men, wouldn't allow a woman to have the floor. Lucretia stood outside the convention hall and spoke anyway. It was outside that convention hall that she met Elizabeth Cady Stanton.

When they returned to the United States, they decided to organize their own convention. The Seneca Falls Convention was the first women's rights conference in the United States. They put out an advertisement in the *Seneca County Courier* on July 11 and 14, 1848, that read, "A Convention to discuss the social, civil, and religious condition and rights of women will be held in the Wesleyan Chapel, at Seneca Falls, New York, on Wednesday and Thursday, the 19th and 20th of July, current; commencing at 10 o'clock a.m. During the first day, the meeting will be exclusively for women, who are earnestly invited to attend. The public generally are invited to be present on the second day, when Lucretia Mott, of Philadelphia, and other ladies and gentlemen, will address the convention."

More than two hundred women showed up that first day,

more than Lucretia and Elizabeth had ever hoped for.

Elizabeth wrote an equal rights version of the Declaration of Independence because the original did not include women. Her version read: "We hold these truths to be self-evident: that all men and women are created equal; that they are endowed by their Creator with certain inalienable rights. . . ."

On the second day, even more women attended the conference. In addition more than forty men, who were supportive of women's rights, attended, including antislavery activist Frederick Douglass.

The convention was mocked by some who believed that women would never get the right to vote, but the momentum of that gathering was unstoppable. An even larger gathering of women occurred two weeks later in Rochester, New York. And an annual women's convention became a regular event in the women's rights movement.

Lucretia and Elizabeth had turned the tide. Lucretia said, "If our principles are right, why should we be cowards?" *Mental Improvement*, the book she had read as a child, was always on her mind.

At that time, women couldn't attend men's colleges. Black students couldn't attend colleges with white students. Lucretia wanted a place where students of all backgrounds could be educated together, where they might read the same books and together go forth and change the world.

The college she cofounded was called Swarthmore, and to this day, it's still considered one of the finest colleges in America: young men and women learning side by side, Americans of all races welcomed through its doors.

#RESIST LESSON

THE BOOKS WE READ CAN CHANGE OUR LIVES—AND THE WORLD.

IDA B. WELLS
#resist 1892

"THE PEOPLE MUST KNOW BEFORE THEY CAN ACT, AND THERE IS NO EDUCATOR TO COMPARE WITH THE PRESS."

WHEN IDA WELLS WAS JUST a baby, Abraham Lincoln issued the Emancipation Proclamation, freeing the enslaved people living in the United States. Ida was six months old—which meant she was born a slave but did not grow up as one. That made all the difference.

Those years after slavery, known as the Reconstruction era, were *very* difficult for black Americans. The South had fought, and many of its men had died, to protect the institution of slavery upon which its economy had been built. They had little practice in seeing black people as fellow human beings with basic human rights when just a short time ago, a white man could *own* a black person and make him work on the farm much the same way one might own a farm animal, like a horse or a cow.

Though the law now forbade it, many white Southerners continued to treat blacks like animals.

When she was a young schoolteacher in Memphis, Ida experienced the brutality of the Reconstruction era firsthand. She was riding in the ladies' car of a train when a white conductor insisted she give up the seat she had paid for. She refused. She had purchased a first-class ticket for the ladies' car and did not want to ride in the crowded smoking car at the back of the train.

The conductor and two other white men dragged her from the train. It was violent. It was wrong. Ida refused to accept the discriminatory treatment.

She wrote about her ordeal for *The Living Way,* a black church weekly. Her article was read all through the city of Memphis and beyond. People of all colors agreed that the way Ida had been treated was *not right.* She brought a lawsuit against the railroad—and won!

Although a higher court would later overturn the case against the railway company, Ida learned a lesson she would carry with her for the rest of her life. When she wrote the truth—the who, what, where, when, and how of a situation—justice was within her grasp.

More, there was no judge or jury who could overturn her writing. She decided to become a journalist.

There were harder days ahead. Ida's friend Thomas Moss opened a grocery store in a black neighborhood. White business owners did not want the competition. A white mob stormed Thomas's store. Thomas and two other black men were arrested and, later, murdered.

Ida was heartbroken. She wrote about it in her newspaper, the *Free Speech and Headlight.* Her words—the truth—made the white Southern community very afraid. They set the newspapers' office on fire and made threats on Ida's life.

Evil thrives in silence.

Ida B. Wells refused to be silenced.

She kept writing and investigating.

The road got rougher ahead.

Ida began to make a connection between the violent murders of black men and women and the rise in black-owned businesses. She was one of the first journalists to declare that lynching, the murder of blacks without a trial or proper legal redress, was about both race *and* money.

She traveled throughout the South documenting case after case. It was dangerous work, investigating the deaths of so many innocent people. Ida once wrote, "I feel . . . utterly discouraged, and just now, if it were possible, would gather my race in my arms and fly away with them."

Every hero has a moment of despair. But it's okay to be discouraged. It's okay to think of turning your back, of running and flying away. There is no one who has acted with courage and did not tremble as they stood in the face of danger.

Ida had that thought, then let it pass. She continued to travel, to document, to *dig* in an effort to uncover the truth.

Reporters have the ability to connect the dots between events, to prove truths that we might not normally see in our everyday lives. When they write about what they've witnessed and draw those connections, there can be a mighty reaction.

Ida's report, "Southern Horrors: Lynch Law in All Its Phases," outraged white Southerners who did not want the world to know how many black people, some of them just children, had been killed in the shadows, where the rage of racism operated without censure.

But it also brought lynching to the attention of readers nationwide who organized against the brutal practice.

Ida's gift to us is the reminder that our words matter. Injustice is weakened the minute you bear witness to it by writing it down. As Ida herself said, "The way to right wrongs is to turn the light of truth upon them."

#RESIST LESSON

INJUSTICE THRIVES IN SILENCE. WHEN WE SPEAK AND WRITE OUR TRUTH, THINGS CHANGE.

MOHANDAS GANDHI

#resist 1906

"THE WEAK CAN NEVER FORGIVE. FORGIVENESS IS THE ATTRIBUTE OF THE STRONG."

BY THE TIME GANDHI WAS born, the British crown had ruled his native land of India for over a decade.

Whenever the people of India tried to fight back, the British sent more armies. People perished. Fighting violence with violence had not been successful.

Gandhi's mother followed the Hindu religion and Ghandi himself was influenced by another religion called Jainism, both of which revere self-discipline and nonviolence.

As a child, Gandhi was shy and not a very good student. But he took his mother's lessons with him when he went to study in London. He thought about her commitment to nonviolence when he endured racial attacks.

He followed her practice of self-discipline by being a vegetarian in a time and a place when choosing to not eat meat made him an outcast.

In his twenties, Gandhi was offered a position as a lawyer in South Africa. He moved there with his wife and his children.

In South Africa, the racial attacks continued.

When he refused to give up his train seat for a European customer, the white conductor beat him up.

Gandhi decided that he would not fight back with his fists but instead organize the people into a series of nonviolent protests.

He came up with the idea of a nonviolent resistance that he called *satyagraha,* which means a "firm loyalty to truth." People often thought about nonviolent resistance as being passive, but Gandhi wanted people to understand that *satyagraha* did not mean that one was weak or giving in. Rather, those who practiced nonviolent resistance could draw upon the strength of truth and justice to face whatever battles lay before them.

He wrote: "Truth (*satya*) implies love, and firmness (*agraha*) engenders and therefore serves as a synonym for force. I thus began to call the Indian movement *Satyagraha,* that is to say, the Force which is born of Truth and Love or non-violence. . . . I have also called it love-force or soul-force."

When the South African government, led by General Jan Christian Smuts, announced a new series of laws that would severely impinge on the rights of Indian citizens, Gandhi knew that this was the time for him to try *satyagraha* on a larger scale.

Beginning in 1906, he led a campaign of civil disobedience. Hundreds of Indians, including Gandhi, were arrested for protesting and spent time in jail. But after eight long years they were triumphant.

The world took notice of Gandhi's action, and General Smuts was forced to back down. *Satyagraha,* truth and firmness, prevailed.

He negotiated a compromise with Smuts that included important repeals of the previously passed laws. The South African government would honor Hindu marriages, and Indians would not be charged a discriminatory poll tax—a fee that had to be paid in order to vote. When Gandhi left the country in 1914, Smuts remarked, "The saint has left our shores, I sincerely hope forever."

Mohandas Gandhi would go on to use the practice of nonviolent protest in a nearly thirty-year resistance in support of Indian independence. On July 18, 1947, the Indian Independence Act was passed. Gandhi and his people were, after more than two centuries of colonialism, finally free.

It was not that Gandhi did not get angry. He was human. We all get angry. But as he told his grandson Arun, anger is not the problem—it's what you choose to do with it that can lead to evil. "I am glad to see you can be moved to anger. Anger is good. I get angry all the time. . . . I have learned to use my anger for good. Anger to people is like gas to the automobile—it fuels you to move forward and get to a better place. Without it we would not be motivated to rise to a challenge. It is an energy that compels us to define what is just and unjust."

If he had picked up a gun and tried to match his oppressors bullet for bullet, he would surely have lost. But when the world saw a man using words instead of his fists, they paid attention. When he chose love in the face of so much hate, hearts softened and people were moved.

It took a long time, a very long time, for these tactics to shift the tides of oppression that had been swelling for hundreds of years.

But Gandhi taught the world that while blind anger and violence can win a battle, love and nonviolence can and will win the war.

#RESIST LESSON

YOU DON'T HAVE TO USE YOUR FISTS.

EMILIANO ZAPATA

#resist 1911

"I'D RATHER DIE ON MY FEET THAN LIVE ON MY KNEES."

WHEN EMILIANO ZAPATA WAS JUST seventeen years old, his parents died, leaving him an orphan. He found a family in the people of his village, Anenecuilco, in Mexico. He would live with them and fight for them his whole life long.

He could have focused just on himself. Emiliano Zapata knew more than how to farm the land: he was also a skilled horseman who earned money at rodeos, who did bullfighting from horseback. He could have taken those skills, made a living, and not bothered with anyone else. But when Porfirio Díaz, the newly elected president of Mexico, began taking land from the peasants, Emiliano Zapata and his band of rebels began to fight back.

Under Díaz's rule, wealthy plantation owners and foreign investors were able to seize huge plots of land called haciendas; and rural farmers, called campesinos, were displaced and thrust even further into poverty.

The wealthy elite were ruthless in their quest to take the farmers' land. Once, in response to the farmworkers' protests, the landowners set fire to an entire village.

Emiliano kept protesting because he believed that land was life. When families could own a piece of land, they could feed their children, be productive members of their community, and make a path for the next generation. He believed that when the land was grabbed and poor farmers became tenants, always in debt and never able to get ahead, the balance of society was thrown off—often permanently.

Emiliano was clever, and sometimes he was able to use his research skills to find the ancient title deeds that proved the true ownership of the land. He would take those deeds to the local governors and implore them to do the right thing.

But the governors were beholden to the corrupt government, and they were slow to act. Sometimes even after Emiliano had presented the case with all the proof in the world, they still would not help the poor campesinos.

Emiliano grew impatient with petitioning the government and began to resist. He took the land away from the plantation owners, redistributing it to the people he believed had been wronged.

In 1910, President Díaz ran for office against a man named Francisco Madero.

Emiliano met with Madero. The two men did not agree about everything, but Madero promised to help the poor people in the rural areas get back the land that was being stolen from them.

To help Madero's campaign, the men who followed Emiliano united as an army. They were called Zapatistas. Emiliano had a new title. He was now officially the general of the Ejército Libertador del Sur, the Liberation Army of the South. Emiliano and his army were a critical force in defeating President Díaz in a hard-fought revolution.

Francisco Madero became the next president of Mexico. But once he was in office, he began to go back on his promises to the people.

Madero tried to buy Emiliano's loyalty by offering him great sums of money to buy a hacienda of his own.

Emiliano refused. His loyalty was to the campesinos—the farmers and the poor, hardworking people of the village.

Madero installed a governor who would support the wealthy plantation owners.

But Emiliano was not done fighting.

He came up with the Plan of Ayala, which stated that Madero was not fit to be president because he did not uphold the ideals of the people who had fought so hard to bring him into office.

Under the Plan of Ayala, Emiliano and the Zapatistas would continue the Mexican Revolution until two democratic terms were met:

A provisional president would be installed until fair elections could be held.

The provisional government would agree to return at least one-third of the land that had been stolen from the poor.

Emiliano's battle cry for the Plan of Ayala was *Tierra y Libertad* ("Land and Liberty").

The people of Mexico saw Emiliano in two very different ways. To the rich he was a renegade bandit, robbing them of the expansion they saw as their right. To the poor he was a hero, a modern-day Robin Hood who helped them retrieve what was rightfully theirs.

But when he cried out *Tierra y Libertad,* he didn't mean just *his* land and *his* liberty. He could have saved himself, but that never crossed his mind.

#RESIST LESSON

WE MUST SPEAK FOR THE VOICELESS.

DIETRICH BONHOEFFER

#resist 1933

"THE CHURCH . . . MUST NOT SIMPLY BANDAGE THE VICTIMS UNDER THE WHEEL OF OPPRESSION, BUT PUT A SPOKE IN THE WHEEL ITSELF."

HE CONSIDERED RUNNING FROM THE problem.

When the Nazis grew in power in his native Germany, Dietrich Bonhoeffer, a young pastor, left Berlin and took a job at a German church in London. He had studied in New York and worked in Barcelona. He had an international community of friends and colleagues that would have helped and supported him. But in London, he did not feel the peace and security he had hoped for. Horrible things were happening in Germany. He needed to go back home.

Back in Berlin, he formed the Confessing Church, a group that openly protested the practices of Nazism. He recruited theological students in hopes of opening their minds and hearts to the trouble at hand. But the Gestapo, the secret police, watched him closely, and eventually the Confessing Church was forced to shut down.

He got a teaching job in New York City at Union Theological Seminary, far away from Germany, the Nazis, and Adolf Hitler's reign. But once he got to the United States, he realized that he could never live with himself if the only safety he'd managed to secure was his own. A month after his arrival, he gave up his position in New York and returned to Germany, where he threw himself into the underground resistance.

Dietrich soon became what he had never imagined when he was a young theology student studying at seminary: a spy.

He got a job at the Abwehr, Germany's military intelligence service, working against the Gestapo from inside their own operation. He helped evacuate Jewish refugees. He siphoned off funds to help them start new lives in safer places.

He considered running away, but instead he came back to help the most vulnerable citizens of his country escape to freedom.

#RESIST LESSON

THE INSTINCT TO RUN AWAY IS NATURAL. IT'S HOW WE RESPOND TO THAT INSTINCT THAT DEFINES OUR COURAGE.

CHIUNE SUGIHARA
#resist 1940

"I DIDN'T DO ANYTHING SPECIAL. . . . I MADE MY OWN DECISIONS, THAT'S ALL. I FOLLOWED MY OWN CONSCIENCE AND LISTENED TO IT."

CHIUNE SUGIHARA WAS BORN IN Japan on the first day of a new era: January 1, 1900.

In that time, and in that place, the individual was expected to put himself, and his own needs, traits, and desires, beneath those of the whole. As a famous Japanese proverb says, "The nail that sticks out gets hammered down."

But Chiune seemed destined to stick out. His father wanted him to study medicine, but Chiune, who longed to live abroad, wanted to study English. He had the same argument with his father over and over again.

Then one day, Chiune decided to end the arguments once

and for all. When the time came to take the medical school exams, he resisted. He walked in, wrote his name on the sheet of paper, and then walked right back out. He deliberately failed. He sat outside the school and ate his lunch. His father was furious, but he was free. He studied English at Waseda University. Being bilingual would enable him to fulfill his dream of working abroad.

Chiune was eighteen when he passed the Japanese Foreign Service exam. For decades he served his country. During World War II, he was placed in Lithuania, a location that made it possible for him to use his position to help Jewish citizens and refugees escape from the Nazis. But the Japanese had strict rules about granting visas, and few of the Jews who crowded his office met the criteria. Chiune wondered: Did he have the strength to once again be the nail that sticks out?

In the summer of 1940, he began granting visas on his own, without the permission of his government's home office. For twenty hours a day, he handwrote visas—processing in hours what might normally take a month.

The Nazis were invading. His office was shutting down. But Chiune kept writing visas. The government sent him orders to come home, and even as he sat in the back seat of a taxi on the way to the train station, Chiune wrote visas.

As the train pulled out of the station and Jewish refugees chased after it, Chiune wrote and signed visas, throwing them out the window until not a single slip of paper was left.

At home, he was punished for his actions. He lost his job. He was forced to support his family selling light bulbs door-to-door.

Not until many years later would he learn that over six thousand Jews escaped the Nazis because of his visas.

Because he dared to be the nail that stuck out, more than forty thousand descendants of those refugees are alive today.

#RESIST LESSON

SOMETIMES YOU MUST BREAK THE RULES TO DO WHAT'S RIGHT.

HEDY LAMARR
#resist 1942

"HOPE AND CURIOSITY ABOUT THE FUTURE SEEMED BETTER THAN GUARANTEES. THAT'S THE WAY I WAS. THE UNKNOWN WAS ALWAYS SO ATTRACTIVE TO ME . . . AND STILL IS."

AS A GIRL, SHE WALKED the woods of Vienna with her father. He was curious about everything, and together they would have long discussions about topics ranging from printing presses to streetcars. He taught her to love the questions, to dig underneath everything she saw, if only with her mind.

When she grew up, she became an actress. The Hollywood movie studio where she worked, MGM, declared her to be "the most beautiful woman in the world." She never really cared about surface beauty, declaring, "Any girl can be glamorous. All you have to do is stand still and look stupid."

In the midst of World War II, she wanted to do something to help the fight against the Nazis. She had always been a tinkerer. She had always been someone who loved questions. She asked her friend George Antheil to help her with an invention.

Together, they created a device that would jam radio signals using a technique called frequency hopping. They patented the device they created, using mini–piano rolls, and gave it to the US Navy.

A glamorous movie star or a brilliant scientist? Which was she? Hedy resisted being put in a box, expected to fulfill only a single, limited role. Her invention wasn't used during World War II. But by the 1960s, Hedy's frequency hopping technology was standard in all military communications.

She never made much money from her invention. Money was never the point. What made her happy, what made her come to life, was pushing her brain as far as it could go.

Today we all carry a little bit of Hedy's genius around in our phones, tablets, and other devices. The ability to frequency hop is what makes it possible for information networks to handle large volumes of cell phone calls and other forms of wireless communication.

Hedy Lamarr was the first woman to receive the BULBIE Gnass Spirit of Achievement Award for "inventions that have significantly contributed to society."

As beautiful as Hedy Lamarr was, her face was nothing

compared with her mind. Her mind was one of the most beautiful in the world.

#RESIST LESSON

EVERY SOLUTION BEGINS WITH THE QUESTION "WHAT IF?"

NELSON MANDELA

#resist 1944

"I LEARNED THAT COURAGE WAS NOT THE ABSENCE OF FEAR, BUT THE TRIUMPH OVER IT. THE BRAVE MAN IS NOT HE WHO DOES NOT FEEL AFRAID, BUT HE WHO CONQUERS THAT FEAR."

HE DID NOT START OUT wanting to be political. He did not know he would one day become president of his country.

When Nelson Mandela was young, he loved ballroom dancing and the theater.

He was a long-distance runner and an amateur boxer. He loved gardening.

As he was growing up in South Africa, a system of oppression was also rising. The system was called apartheid, and it formalized and legalized discrimination against an entire race of people. Blacks were the majority in South Africa, but the white minority ruled. Apartheid codified that rule and made it law.

As Nelson got older, he joined the African National Congress, an organization formed to advocate for the voting rights of all citizens and to end apartheid. He did not imagine a life in politics. He wanted only fair treatment for himself and his race.

When he was arrested in 1962, the world watched as he was taken off to prison. It was in prison that Mandela's waiting—and winning—began. He resisted by becoming the international symbol of the injustice of apartheid. The South African government, feeling the pressure from the international community, offered Mandela deals in exchange for his freedom. He refused.

Each time the government approached him, he refused.

He knew that a farmer need not always be present for his seeds to grow. He knew that while he was on the inside, the antiapartheid work continued outside. Eventually the minority government was forced to topple. Mandela was released in 1990, and he began the difficult work of mending all that had been broken in the democracy of South Africa.

In 1994, he was elected president, but he did not use his power to punish. Rather, he sought peace, becoming a symbol of hope and justice for people all around the world.

#RESIST LESSON

WE DO NOT NEED TO SEE OURSELVES AS HEROES TO CHANGE THE WORLD.

OSKAR SCHINDLER
#resist 1945

"I HATED THE BRUTALITY, THE SADISM AND THE INSANITY OF NAZISM. I JUST COULDN'T STAND BY AND SEE PEOPLE DESTROYED. I DID WHAT I COULD, WHAT I HAD TO DO, WHAT MY CONSCIENCE TOLD ME I MUST DO. THAT'S ALL THERE IS TO IT. REALLY. NOTHING MORE."

OSKAR SCHINDLER NEVER THOUGHT HE was cut out to be a hero. When he was sixteen, he was expelled for forging his report card. He graduated high school but never went to college.

As a young man, he bounced from job to job. When he was thirty-one, Adolf Hitler and the Nazi Party ruled Germany. The world was at war and the Nazis had begun systematically imprisoning and murdering Jews throughout Europe. At the time, Oskar owned two factories in Poland.

When the Nazis came to Poland, Oskar Schindler tried to protect the hundreds of Jewish workers who worked at his factory. At first he used bribes, diplomacy, and his wiles—the same ones that got him into trouble in school. When he heard that the Nazis were planning a raid on the Jewish ghetto in Kraków, for example, he protected his workers by letting them sleep in the factory overnight.

The Nazis caught on to Oskar Schindler's tricks eventually. Three times he was arrested and accused of using his business to protect the Jews. Three times he fought against his imprisonment and was set free.

Many in his country saw how dangerous the Nazis were. They began to turn a blind eye to the crimes being committed against the Jewish people. Oskar didn't have to get involved. He had an easy way out. He was not Jewish. He could have sold his factories and returned to his home in Moravia, which is a part of the current Czech Republic. Simply put, he could have walked away and been—in a sense—free.

But Oskar saw that he had a chance to save lives. More than that, he felt an obligation to try, even if it meant facing prison—or worse.

Oskar had to decide what was greater—the punishment he might face for doing what he *knew* was right or the pain he would live with knowing that he had allowed others to suffer and die. Oskar could not live with the pain of not trying.

He decided to relocate his factories to Moravia. He and his assistant drew up a list of twelve hundred Jews they could hire at the factory. This became known as "Schindler's List." With that list, Oskar Schindler was able to take eight hundred men and four hundred women to Moravia, saving them from the Nazi concentration camps.

One man saved twelve hundred people. It's a staggering number, but the important thing to remember is that Oskar Schindler believed that if he could save only one life, it would be worth the risk. We are measured not by the results of our actions but by the courage that compels us to act.

#RESIST LESSON

WHOEVER SAVES ONE LIFE SAVES THE WORLD ENTIRE.

THE DALAI LAMA
#resist 1959

"IF YOU THINK YOU ARE TOO SMALL TO MAKE A DIFFERENCE, TRY SLEEPING WITH A MOSQUITO."

HE WAS ONLY FOUR YEARS old when he was officially named "His Holiness, the 14th Dalai Lama," the spiritual leader of the Tibetan people. He'd been identified, at the age of two, as the reincarnation of his predecessor, the 13th Dalai Lama.

In the Tibetan tradition, the dalai lamas are the living embodiments of the bodhisattva, a being of tremendous compassion. Once he was chosen to be the next Dalai Lama, he was taught to put others first: to open his mind and his heart to everyone he encountered.

He began training to lead his people when he was six years old. As a child, he sometimes resented not being able to have the same kind of carefree fun that other kids did. He spent most of his time in a monastery, a religious community. He had playmates, but most of them were adults. When asked if he had ever thought about being a normal person instead of the Dalai Lama, he replied, "Yes, at a young age. Sometimes I felt, 'Oh, this is a burden. I wish I was an unknown Tibetan. Then I'd have more freedom.' But then later I realized that my position was something useful to others."

He spent a lot of his days in quiet: reading and meditating. He still does.

He believes that in the quiet, people find peace—and that inner peace is something we should all strive for. He said, "If every eight-year-old is taught meditation, we will eliminate violence from the world within one generation."

When he was just fifteen years old, he was named the leader of his country.

Can you imagine being a teenager and being in charge of a country of six million people?

When he was twenty-four, he took exams at three academically focused monasteries: Drepung, Sera, and Ganden. One morning he was examined by thirty scholars on logic. In the afternoon, he debated with fifteen scholars on the subject of moderation known as the Middle Path, and in the evening, thirty-five scholars tested his knowledge of the canon of monastic discipline and the study of metaphysics. He passed his exams with full honors and received a Geshe Lharampa degree (doctorate of Buddhist philosophy) when he was twenty-five.

He was still in the midst of his studies when Tibet was invaded by China. In 1954, he traveled to China to meet with Mao Zedong and other Chinese leaders. He hoped for a peaceful reconciliation, but the Chinese were determined to incorporate Tibet as part of their nation.

In 1959, he was forced into exile.

The Dalai Lama spent many years fighting for the independence of his country. He made multiple appeals to the United Nations for Tibetan democracy and independence, but the Chinese occupation continued and still continues today.

Being a leader in exile for most of his life has made him realize how deeply people are connected, how borders are illusory. Since he cannot go home to Tibet, he has brought Tibet to the world.

In his speeches, he reminds the world that we have a better chance of achieving a peaceful world if we embrace the Tibetan idea of "universal responsibility." He urges people to pay less attention to nations and borders and more to a commitment to be helpful and to do right, in whatever small way we can.

He devotes himself to the launching of institutions—educational, cultural, and religious—that preserve Tibetan identity and heritage all over the world. In this way—not through war or violence—the Dalai Lama resists. Despite the military force occupying his country, he keeps Tibet alive.

Nearly eighty thousand refugees followed the Dalai Lama

into exile. He created a school to teach them the language, history, and culture of their country.

He founded the Library of Tibetan Works and Archives, which houses more than one hundred thousand manuscripts and documents about Tibetan history, politics, and life.

He gives speeches, and what he begins to talk about is not politics but kindness. This, he says, is his religion.

He could have made his time in exile one of darkness and silence. It has been more than fifty years since he has been allowed to visit his home country of Tibet.

But rather than focus on all that he and his people have lost, he has chosen to share his wisdom, often tinged with humor, with the world.

He often shares a popular Tibetan saying: "Wherever you have friends, that's your country, and wherever you receive love, that's your home."

At the end of the twentieth century and into the twenty-first century, when wars reigned and people suffered, he has become a symbol of hope and optimism for the world.

It isn't that he never gets angry. When asked if he ever felt rage, he once said, "Oh, yes, of course. I'm a human being. Generally speaking, if a human being never shows anger, then I think something's wrong. He's not right in the brain." (Then he laughed.)

When asked about how he stayed hopeful in the face of great tragedy, he said, "I always look at any event from a wider angle. There's always some problem, some killing, some murder or terrorist act or scandal everywhere, every day. But if you think the whole world is like that, you're wrong. Out of six billion humans, the troublemakers are just a handful."

He believes that we are more alike than not. He reminds us that good people far outnumber those who commit acts of cruelty and injustice.

He urges us to imagine the other person's point of view, to remember that we are more connected than we might imagine.

He wants us to know that even when we don't always understand each other, it helps to remember that deep down, we all want happiness and that the world is a better place when we look upon other people's suffering as a burden we might share.

It all comes down to sharing, he believes.

Share the suffering.

Share the joy.

Change the world.

#RESIST LESSON

THE PEOPLE WHO WANT TO DO GOOD ARE THE REAL MAJORITY. TROUBLEMAKERS MAKE UP JUST A HANDFUL OF ALL THE PEOPLE IN THE WORLD.

DOLORES HUERTA AND CESAR CHAVEZ

#resist 1962

"CHERISH YOUR HERITAGE. THE HARVEST IS GREAT."

DOLORES HUERTA AND CESAR CHAVEZ shared a vision: to organize the farmworkers who picked the fruits and vegetables that fed our nation. And to help those people, and their families, have a better life.

Together, they founded the National Farm Workers Association, now called the United Farm Workers of America.

People said that although they loved each other, Dolores and Cesar could fight like brother and sister. They embraced their differences. They encouraged each other to speak up whenever one of them disagreed. How could they be strong in the face of all their challenges if they didn't have the courage to be honest with each other?

Dolores proved to be a shrewd lobbyist and negotiator. She fought for and won the right for farmworkers to collect aid for their families and disability insurance when they were hurt on their job—something they could never do before.

She helped elect President Bill Clinton, Congressman Ron Dellums, Governor Jerry Brown, Congresswoman Hilda Solis, and Senator Hillary Rodham Clinton.

Dolores knew how to help connect people across the issues that mattered most—and she helped teach a generation that one of the most valuable things they owned was their vote.

Together, Cesar and Dolores organized the Salad Bowl strike of 1970, the largest farmworker strike in American history. This was where Cesar did some of his most powerful work: he was great on the ground, connecting with the people.

The national boycott of California table grapes brought Dolores to New York, and there she got to know Gloria Steinem and members of the modern women's rights movement. It hadn't occurred to her how much she was a role model to young women. She began to be an even louder voice for gender equality in the farmworkers' movement.

It was Dolores and Cesar who first began the national use of the phrase *Sí, se puede*: "Yes, we can." The phrase ended up being the slogan of Barack Obama's historic presidential campaign. But years before, it was just Dolores and Cesar sitting across from each other in a tiny office, encouraging each other that they could do what nobody had ever done before: shine a spotlight on the farmworkers of America and, in the process, transform the lives and legacy of millions of families for generations to come.

#RESIST LESSON

HONOR THE HANDS THAT HARVEST YOUR CROPS.

FANNIE LOU HAMER
#resist 1962

"THERE IS ONE THING YOU HAVE GOT TO LEARN ABOUT OUR MOVEMENT. THREE PEOPLE ARE BETTER THAN NO PEOPLE."

BY THE TIME SHE WAS thirteen years old, Fannie Lou Hamer had dropped out of school to help her parents on the farm where they worked. Slavery had ended, but the plantations didn't disappear. Crops still needed to be sown, tended, and harvested, and many African Americans remained in the South to do the job, under a system called sharecropping. In it, landowners would take a portion of profits from farmers who used their land.

Though black men and women were then technically free, a complex system of laws known as "Jim Crow" sprang up in the

South to keep black people from exercising their freedoms—including their right to vote.

Fannie Lou Hamer was a young woman in the Jim Crow era. She registered to vote, and once she did, she dedicated her life to making sure that she, and anyone who wanted to vote, actually could.

Fannie was one of eighteen volunteers who went to register to vote at the Indianola Courthouse in Mississippi. She pretended she couldn't read or write to see what would happen. The white Southerners staffing the voting booths gave her a test. There was no such test for white voters, no matter whether they could read or not. When Fannie failed the test, they refused to allow her to vote. That was illegal.

That night, on the way home, the volunteers' bus was stopped and they were fined $100. The police officer said they were driving a bus of "the wrong color," a completely made-up infraction and a clear attempt to keep black Americans from traveling to the polls to vote together. That was also illegal.

The freedom of African Americans was being restricted. The message from white people in power was clear: *Stop protesting. Stop trying to make your voices heard. You are not wanted. You are not valued.*

When Fannie got back to the farm where she worked, she was fired for trying to vote. Fannie continued to press for change so that black Americans could exercise their constitutional rights.

It was a years-long struggle.

She was arrested.

Beaten.

Shot at. Seventeen times.

She was forced for a time to go into hiding.

But Fannie Lou Hamer became only more determined. It said a lot about the power of voting that some people were willing to go so far to keep their fellow citizens away from the polls. Every time they tried to stop her, Fannie grew surer of her work's importance.

She began to give speeches, and everywhere she went, she moved people with her words. She didn't have a fancy education. But when she spoke, it was straightforward and from the heart—and people listened. Everyone from the farms of Mississippi to the executive office of the White House would come to know the name Fannie Lou Hamer.

In 1964, a summer that activists dubbed Freedom Summer because of their unrelenting work toward passing the Civil Rights Act, Fannie Lou Hamer went to Atlantic City, New Jersey.

She and the other members of what they called the Mississippi Freedom Democratic Party challenged the Mississippi delegation at the Democratic National Convention and asked to be seated at the convention.

President Lyndon B. Johnson was so terrified of Fannie's powerful testimony that he held an impromptu press conference to distract the national television stations from Fannie's speech.

But Johnson's tactic did not work. That night, every prime-time news show carried coverage of Fannie's testimony. Her words traveled from television stations to living rooms across America.

In her most famous speech, Fannie let the world know that she "was sick and tired of being sick and tired." Picking cotton was tiring. Working on a sweltering plantation for pennies a day was sickening. But the black community's continuing struggle to simply be seen as valuable—as *equal*—was intolerable. Fannie never stopped pushing, speaking, and marching. She was taking her place in the march of history. It was a long time coming, but a change was going to come.

Fannie Lou Hamer stood for justice. She stood for democracy. She reminded us of all we have been given, every time we walk into an election booth and vote.

#RESIST LESSON

OUR VOTE IS ONE OF THE MOST VALUABLE THINGS WE OWN.

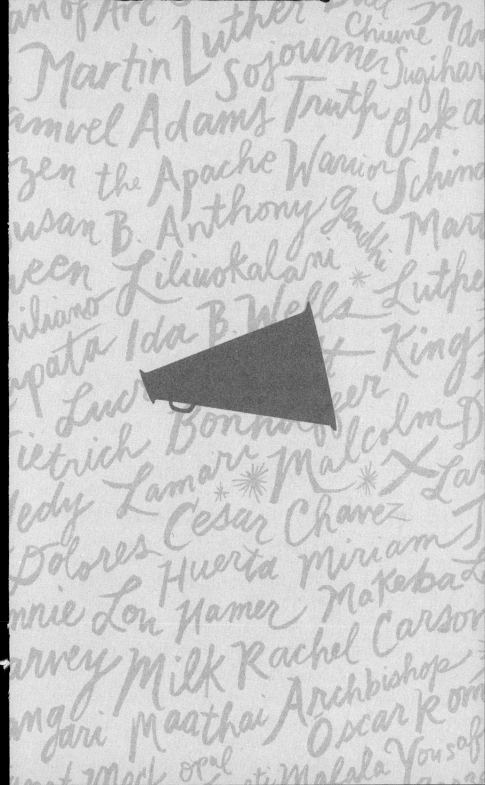

RACHEL CARSON
#resist 1962

"ONE WAY TO OPEN YOUR EYES IS TO ASK YOURSELF, 'WHAT IF I HAD NEVER SEEN THIS BEFORE? WHAT IF I KNEW I WOULD NEVER SEE IT AGAIN?'"

SHE GREW UP ON HER family's farm in Pennsylvania, near the Allegheny River. She published her first story when she was ten years old. To her the natural world, from the forest to the oceans and everywhere in between, was a palace of treasures just waiting to be discovered. When she was out exploring, she was always happy. When she leaned down and felt something as simple as a ladybug crawling on her arm, she felt like a part of something.

She said, "Those who dwell . . . among the beauties and mysteries of the earth are never alone or weary of life."

In college, she fell in love with oceanography, the study of the seas. She studied at the famous Marine Biological Laboratory in Woods Hole, Massachusetts. Her first job was writing radio scripts for a show about the ocean called *Romance under the Waters*. For Rachel Carson, her feeling for the ocean *was* a romance, a love affair she'd have her whole life.

She became the second woman scientist hired at the US Bureau of Fisheries. She was proud of the title that hung on her office door: Junior Aquatic Biologist.

Rachel's love of nature and fascination with our planet continued throughout her life. In 1939, the US Bureau of Fisheries became part of the newly created US Fish and Wildlife Service. As an official there, Rachel started to study something she believed would do more harm than good to the plants and the trees around us. It was a pesticide called DDT. A pesticide is something farmers use to keep insects from eating the crops. DDT was known as "the insect bomb" in part because the recent atomic bombing of Hiroshima and Nagasaki were still fresh in the headlines. The idea was that DDT eradicated bugs the way an atomic bomb eradicated each of those cities.

Rachel was one of the first people to say that DDT would hurt both human beings and animals, especially birds. She believed that DDT caused cancer—and she was right.

In 1962, she published her groundbreaking book, *Silent Spring.*

Rachel's book didn't just change the use of pesticides. It

made the entire country look at how we were treating the earth, making her one of the first environmentalists of the modern age.

The problem with environmentalism, of course, is that it can slow down or even stop the work of corporations that use the planet's natural resources for profit. Rachel's discovery about DDT could cost government agencies and big corporations millions of dollars. They would have to slow down—change the way they did business. They would have to take better care of the environment.

The chemical companies went after Rachel Carson. They started a smear campaign against her, claiming that she was a crazy "woman scientist" who didn't know what she was talking about.

But when Rachel appeared on a *CBS Reports* television special, Americans were able to see that she was not, as her critics had claimed, a "hysterical alarmist." The American people shifted their attention to the unregulated use of pesticides, and a short time later, a congressional review of pesticide dangers was ordered. Under John F. Kennedy, the President's Science Advisory Committee report was released—and its findings were the same as Rachel's.

Ten years after the publication of *Silent Spring,* the Environmental Protection Agency secured a phase-out plan for DDT in the United States. People often wondered how one woman had the tenacity to take on the biggest corporations and Congress in a battle that had not even been publicly declared. But her courage was not for herself—it was for the world. That made all the difference.

In comic books, cities have superheroes who help them fight the bad guys. The planet Earth had Rachel Carson. She inspired a legion of environmentalists to study the human toll on our earth and seas. Because of her, things were never the same.

#RESISTANCE LESSON

EARTH IS OUR HOME. WHEN WE FIGHT FOR NATURE, WE FIGHT FOR OURSELVES.

JOHN LEWIS
#resist 1963

"WHAT I TRY TO TELL YOUNG PEOPLE IS THAT IF YOU COME TOGETHER WITH A MISSION, AND IT'S GROUNDED WITH LOVE AND A SENSE OF COMMUNITY, YOU CAN MAKE THE IMPOSSIBLE POSSIBLE."

JOHN LEWIS GREW UP IN a segregated Alabama. Black families and white families lived in different neighborhoods. Black children and white children attended different schools. When John tried to get a library card, he couldn't because the library was "whites only."

When he was eleven years old, his uncle took him on a trip to Buffalo, New York.

Buffalo was not segregated.

John said that visiting Buffalo was like "stepping into

a movie, into a strange, otherworldly place . . . the sidewalks crowded with people, black and white alike, mixing together as though it was the most natural thing in the world." John went home to Alabama, but he was never the same.

When John was in high school, the Montgomery bus boycott—started by Rosa Parks and led by Martin Luther King Jr.—was the talk of every dinner table. For more than a year, blacks boycotted the buses—meaning they refused to ride them—because although they paid the same fare as white passengers, they were forced to sit in the back.

John Lewis uses the phrase "good trouble" to describe his form of nonviolent resistance. Roughly, "good trouble" means purposely running afoul of the system to highlight that system's injustice. As a student at Fisk University, John found a lot of ways to get into "good trouble." He helped organize what were called Freedom Rides. In them, he and other students traveled across the South, sitting in seats that were marked "whites only." They were arrested by the police, more than once. They were beaten by anti–civil rights mobs, more than once. John never gave up. He believed that the tide of history would turn—that segregation was an outdated system that would and must fall.

In 1960 John helped form the Student Nonviolent Coordinating Committee (SNCC) and served as its chairman. John was named one of the "Big Six" leaders of the civil rights movement. He was just twenty-three when he helped plan the

March on Washington with Martin Luther King Jr. John was the youngest speaker to take the podium at that historic event.

John endured more than forty arrests, beatings, and grievous injuries, but he never wavered from his philosophy of nonviolent civil disobedience. In 1965, John helped organize a moment that would live in history. He led more than six hundred peaceful protesters over the Edmund Pettus Bridge in Selma, Alabama. Their goal was to walk into the county courthouse and register to vote. On the other side of the bridge, Alabama State Troopers were waiting.

The peaceful protesters were beaten so badly that the day was called "Bloody Sunday." The blood of people who had done no more than walk across the bridge poured in the streets.

John knew that although the mobs and policemen who attacked the protesters seemed powerful, they were acting out of fear and that the march for equality would eventually best that fear.

John's skull was fractured by a policeman's nightstick, but he managed to get away. Before he checked himself into the hospital, he went on TV and implored President Lyndon B. Johnson to come to Alabama. He was hurt. He was in trouble. But it was good trouble.

The world watched Selma through those cameras. Because of the protesters and the journalists who came out, the violent, unconstitutional tactics of segregationists were exposed.

Marching matters.

Holding up a camera to injustice matters.

We can all do our part and get into what John calls some "good trouble."

#RESIST LESSON

FIND A WAY—TO GET IN THE WAY.

MARTIN LUTHER KING JR.
AND
MALCOLM X
#resist 1965

"DARKNESS CANNOT DRIVE OUT DARKNESS;
ONLY LIGHT CAN DO THAT.
HATE CANNOT DRIVE OUT HATE;
ONLY LOVE CAN DO THAT."

—*Martin Luther King Jr.*

MARTIN LUTHER KING JR. AND Malcolm X were major figures in the American civil rights movement. They had the same aim—full and equal rights for black Americans and freedom from racism and oppression—but their approaches to achieving those goals could not have been more different.

Martin was born in an Atlanta, Georgia, neighborhood called Sweet Auburn, into a group of people who believed in being a community and that equality was the holy grail.

As a first-year college student at Morehouse College, Martin was assigned to read an essay that would change his life. It was called "Civil Disobedience," and it was by a man who lived nearly a hundred years before Martin was born, Henry David Thoreau. Thoreau was a New England author, naturalist, abolitionist, and historian. At the time of the essay's writing, the US government was trying to expand its territory into Mexico. With the expansion of territory could have come the expansion of slavery.

In "Civil Disobedience," Thoreau pointed out that slavery thrived not just because of Southern plantation owners, but also because of Northerners who either profited from the agricultural wealth of slavery or were too uninterested to act. Thoreau believed in civil disobedience because he believed that voting, while an important right, was not enough to push change forward. He wrote, "All voting is a sort of gaming, like checkers or backgammon, with a slight moral tinge to it, a playing with right and wrong, with moral questions; and betting naturally accompanies it. The character of the voters is not staked. I cast my vote, perchance, as I think right; but I am not vitally concerned that that right should prevail. I am willing to leave it to the majority. Its obligation, therefore, never exceeds that of expediency. Even voting for the right is doing nothing for it. It is only expressing to men feebly your desire that it should prevail. A wise man will not leave the right to the mercy of chance, nor wish it to prevail through the power of the majority."

Thoreau was so angered by the plans to expand slavery to Mexico that he did not just vote, he took action. He refused to pay his taxes and went to jail rather than support the government's effort to spread the business of slavery.

The actions of Thoreau made a great impression on Martin when he was in college. Martin wrote, "Fascinated by the idea of refusing to cooperate with an evil system, I was so deeply moved that I reread the work several times. I became convinced that noncooperation with evil is as much a moral obligation as is cooperation with good."

When Rosa Parks, then a secretary for the local National Association for the Advancement of Colored People, refused to give up her seat to a white passenger on a Montgomery, Alabama, bus, she was arrested and a movement was launched.

Black residents of Montgomery decided not to ride the buses until the policy of making blacks sit at the back of the bus was rescinded. The bus boycott lasted 381 days, putting economic pressure on both the transportation system and the downtown business owners. Martin was the bus boycott's leader and official spokesperson. He was inspired by the work of Mohandas Gandhi and the activist Bayard Rustin along with Thoreau, and he believed that nonviolent civil disobedience was the most powerful path to change.

Martin shared the work of Thoreau with everyone he knew. In his autobiography, he wrote, "As a result of [Thoreau's] writings and personal witness, we are the heirs of a legacy of creative protest. The teachings of Thoreau came alive in our civil rights movement; indeed, they are more alive than ever before. Whether expressed in a sit-in at lunch counters, a freedom ride into Mississippi, a peaceful protest in Albany, Georgia, a bus boycott in Montgomery, Alabama, these are outgrowths of Thoreau's insistence that evil must be resisted and that no moral man can patiently adjust to injustice."

Martin became a target for white supremacists, who firebombed his home, but he remained steadfast. He founded the Southern Christian Leadership Conference, whose motto was: "Not one hair of one head of one person should be harmed."

Martin Luther King Jr. and his colleagues believed in the words of their contemporary, the poet Audre Lorde: "The master's tools will never dismantle the master's house."

Martin Luther King said, "Nonviolence is a powerful and just weapon, which cuts without wounding and enables the man who weilds it. It is a sword that heals." Not everyone agreed.

"I'M FOR TRUTH, NO MATTER WHO TELLS IT. I'M FOR JUSTICE, NO MATTER WHO IT'S FOR OR AGAINST."

—Malcolm X

HE WAS BORN MALCOLM LITTLE in very different circumstances from those of Martin Luther King Jr. His father was killed when he was six. His mother was in a mental hospital by the time he entered junior high. He bounced from foster home to foster home until trouble came looking for him and he landed in prison. It was there that he discovered the Nation of Islam and he replaced his street ways with structure, discipline, and sense of connection, fostered by his new faith. Malcolm changed his last name to X. He wanted a new identity to reflect his new life.

Malcolm's approach to equal rights was "the ballot or the bullet," meaning that either black Americans would be given equality or they would take it by whatever means necessary. Malcolm, in his early teachings, was not opposed to violence. He spoke of the "white devil" and encouraged his followers to view their white oppressors through this lens—that the white people they encountered were to be shunned.

Though they fought for the same cause, Martin and Malcolm appeared to be polar opposites, two like ends of a magnet that could not exist side by side. But important experiences outside the United States would shape the ideals of both of these men, bringing their seemingly conflicting beliefs closer together than any of their peers would have imagined.

Martin Luther King Jr. traveled to India in 1959. In 1964, Malcolm X traveled to Saudi Arabia, to Mecca.

In India, Martin Luther King met members of Mohandas Gandhi's family and some of his followers. He came back home inspired, more committed to the path of nonviolence than ever before.

King was arrested in 1963, and then he wrote one of his most famous essays, "Letter from Birmingham Jail."

It was both a testimony of admiration for the techniques of Gandhi and a subtle acknowledgment of the role that men such as Malcolm X might play if the country did not shift its stance on civil rights.

King organized the March on Washington for Jobs and Freedom, a peaceful protest that was attended by more than a quarter-million Americans and took place on August 28, 1963. It was there that he gave the most well-known speech of his career, the "I Have a Dream" speech.

The next year, King was awarded a Nobel Peace Prize and

President Lyndon B. Johnson signed the Civil Rights Act of 1964 into law.

In April of 1964, Malcolm X traveled to Mecca to complete a traditional Muslim pilgrimage called a hajj. There, on the road to Mecca, Malcolm said that seeing Muslims of "all colors, from blue-eyed blondes to black-skinned Africans," interacting as equals fundamentally changed his thinking. He returned to the United States, and while the fierce battle for equality still raged, he began speaking to white people about the struggle for equality.

Throughout their lives, both Martin Luther King Jr. and Malcolm X sought to bring freedom, at long last, to their people. Their country was faced with a clear choice in viewing both men. Would Martin's resistance have succeeded without the more radical voice of Malcolm echoing in the background? The world will never know.

Martin and Malcolm met just once, in Washington, DC. Two men of different backgrounds, with very different styles, who were ultimately working toward the same dream: equality.

#RESIST LESSON

IN OUR DIFFERENCES, WE CAN SPUR EACH OTHER TOWARD A COMMON CAUSE.

MIRIAM MAKEBA

#resist 1969

"I LOOK AT AN ANT AND I SEE MYSELF: A NATIVE SOUTH AFRICAN ENDOWED BY NATURE WITH A STRENGTH MUCH GREATER THAN MY SIZE SO I MIGHT COPE WITH THE WEIGHT OF A RACISM THAT CRUSHES MY SPIRIT."

FIRST, CAME THE SIGNS: "FOR use by white persons only." The signs dictated that black citizens in South Africa were not permitted to visit certain beaches, ride specific buses, be treated at "whites only" hospitals, or attend "whites only" schools and colleges.

Then came the laws. People of different colors were not allowed to marry. This was called the Prohibition of Mixed Marriages. Next followed the law that excluded black students from receiving the best education. This was called the Bantu

Education Act. More laws followed.

The system was called "apartheid," the Dutch word for apartness. The laws meant that whites, who formed the National Party, were in power and had all the freedom. Blacks were kept separate, with little opportunity and few freedoms under a government that turned a blind eye to the violence and injustice that black citizens suffered.

Miriam Makeba was just a teenager when these laws went into effect in 1948. She had grown up proud of her black African heritage. Her mother was from the Swazi people, known for their tribal royal heritage. Her father was Xhosa—his people spoke a language that included clicking sounds unusual to Western ears. Miriam took those two heritages, and with all that history she made music.

She was just twenty-three and a member of a pop music group called the Skylarks when she met Nelson Mandela, a young lawyer who would one day become the president of South Africa. When he was imprisoned for fighting against apartheid, Nelson Mandela would say that Miriam's music filled him with hope, each note giving him the strength to push forward into the next day.

When she was twenty-seven, she appeared in her first film, *Come Back, Africa*, a documentary that sought to expose the injustice of apartheid. Miriam traveled to Venice and London to promote the film. The documentary made her an international star.

In London, she met an American singer named Harry Belafonte. He had enjoyed great success in the United States and offered to help Miriam record her own music as a solo artist. She settled in the United States.

Miriam could have recorded whatever she wanted. She chose to perform the music of her people, in English as well as in the African languages of Xhosa and Zulu. Her voice, and the playful rhythms that she brought to the music, signaled the dawn of a powerful new genre called Afro-pop, which melded African music with American and European influences.

Singing original songs such as her big hit, "Pata Pata," Miriam accomplished more than she had ever imagined. Her music made people all over the world dance. But it also made them think.

They listened to her lyrics. They watched her on television. They read interviews with her in newspapers and magazines. Through her music, her voice, everyday people began to understand that the system of "apartheid" did not mean that blacks and whites lived lives that were simply "apart." Black people were dying in South Africa. The white regime held all the wealth and all the power. Families and children were going hungry, with little chance of changing their situation. Because of young activists like Nelson Mandela, but also because of Miriam's music, the world began to question the government of South Africa.

In 1960, a group of blacks protested the injustices of apartheid in a South African township called Sharpeville. There were over five thousand protesters out that day, and in an effort to control them, the white police officers began shooting into the nonviolent crowd. Sixty-nine innocent people died that day in a tragedy that came to be known as the Sharpeville Massacre.

Two of Miriam's relatives were killed in the Sharpeville Massacre, and shortly afterward, her mother passed away. When Miriam tried to return home to attend her mother's funeral, she found that the South African government had revoked her passport. She was no longer permitted to travel to her home country. She would not be permitted to return home for thirty years.

Miriam kept singing. She sang a song in Xhosa called "The Click Song," and audiences were mesmerized. She received a coveted invitation to sing at the birthday of the US president John F. Kennedy. She testified at the United Nations before a special committee for the abolition of apartheid. She became a symbol of African independence for countries throughout the continent.

Because of her courage, because of the beauty of her voice, they called her Mama Afrika. And wherever people fought for freedom, wherever they battled for independence, they played her music.

Nelson Mandela said, "Her haunting melodies gave voice to the pain of exile and dislocation which she felt for thirty-one long years. At the same time, her music inspired a powerful sense of hope in all of us. . . . She was South Africa's first lady of song and so richly deserved the title of Mama Afrika. She was a mother to our struggle and to the young nation of ours."

In February 1990, Nelson Mandela was finally released from prison and the walls of apartheid came crumbling down. Mandela invited Miriam to come to South Africa, and she returned home to the land she had left so many years before. She gathered with some of the greatest musicians of her generation—Dizzy Gillespie, Nina Simone, and Hugh Masekela—and she recorded a new album, the title of which embodied the hope that she had never let go of. The album was called *Eyes on Tomorrow*.

She opened a home for orphans called the Makeba Centre for Girls to tap into the power and possibility that girls have to lead nations and change the world.

Her old friend Nelson Mandela became president.

Miriam had lived to see the impossible become possible. Although she never held elected office, she rang the bell of freedom with her voice. She reminded the world that there is no sweeter song than equality; there is no melody more powerful than the thunderous roar of liberty.

#RESIST LESSON

THE PEOPLE WHO MAKE ART, THE PEOPLE WHO SING SONGS, THEY GIVE HOPE AND SUSTENANCE TO THE RESISTANCE.

HARVEY MILK
#resist 1972

"IT TAKES NO COMPROMISING TO GIVE PEOPLE THEIR RIGHTS. IT TAKES NO MONEY TO RESPECT THE INDIVIDUAL. IT TAKES NO POLITICAL DEAL TO GIVE PEOPLE FREEDOM. IT TAKES NO SURVEY TO REMOVE REPRESSION."

IN HIGH SCHOOL, HARVEY MILK played football and loved the opera. The football was encouraged. The opera? It raised a few eyebrows. People wondered if Harvey might have something . . . wrong with him.

Harvey knew that he was gay, but he never told anyone. Gay people weren't accepted by most of society at that time. Keeping his true self secret made Harvey feel lonely. Homophobia drove the laws and actions of communities, schools, and major institutions. Openly gay people suffered from widespread, and often brutal, legal and social discrimination.

In 1972, he moved to San Francisco. It was a place where people who felt different could feel at home. Harvey lived openly, as a gay man, for the first time. He didn't feel so alone anymore.

San Francisco had become known as the gay mecca, a place where LGBT—lesbians, gays, bisexuals, and transgender people—could live openly and in peace. But widespread acceptance did not come right away. Increased visibility, living openly, meant that early generations of LGBT people faced severe antigay harassment and even violence.

Harvey believed that the women's movement had it right when they said the personal was political. Antigay legislation and the election of officials openly hostile to the gay community were taking place all over the country. Harvey knew gay men and women had to step out of the shadows and make their personal truth known. Otherwise, politicians would never think they needed to reckon with the gay members of their constituency. And they could continue to legislate against them. He urged people to let their loved ones know who they were and what they stood for. In one of his most famous speeches, he said:

> *Gay brothers and sisters . . . You must come out.*
> *Come out . . . to your parents . . . I know that it is*
> *hard and will hurt them but think about how they*

will hurt you in the voting booth! . . . Come out
to your relatives . . . come out to your friends . . .
if indeed they are your friends. Come out to your
neighbors . . . to your fellow workers . . . to the people
who work where you eat and shop . . . come out only
to the people you know, and who know you. Not to
anyone else. But once and for all, break down the
myths, destroy the lies and distortions. For your sake.
For their sake. For the sake of the youngsters who are
becoming scared by the votes from Dade to Eugene.

Homosexual men and women had been forced by society to keep their sexual orientation a secret for so long that this idea of living openly was, to most of the country, a huge act of resistance.

In San Francisco Harvey opened a camera shop and, as a small-business owner, got interested in local politics. He founded the Castro Village Association to help promote LGBT businesses and their owners. (Though the term LGBT would not have been used during Harvey Milk's time.)

Harvey started the Castro Street Fair to bring the crowds to the neighborhood's storefronts. The fair had DJs, food vendors, and artists selling their work. People were literally dancing in the streets. This made Harvey happy. He used the popularity of the fair to raise money for local charities. People had fun, but they also did a lot of good.

The first year, five thousand people came to the fair. Three years later, that number had grown to seventy thousand. Nowadays, more than a quarter of a million people come out each year to the fair that Harvey Milk started. A fair that is, in large part, a celebration of San Francisco's gay population.

Harvey knew that having openly gay citizens hold public office would be one of the most powerful ways to affect change. He said, "There is a major difference . . . between a friend and a gay person, a friend in office and a gay person in office. . . . It's not enough anymore just to have friends represent us. No matter how good that friend may be."

Harvey ran for a San Francisco City/County supervisor seat and lost by the narrowest of margins. But Harvey learned that when it comes to elections, you can't run just once. If you believe in public service, if you're in it to make a difference, you've got to run again.

On his third try, Harvey won the race for that San Francisco City/County supervisor seat and became known as one of the first openly gay elected officials in the United States.

When he was sworn into office, he stood with three other firsts for San Francisco:

Carol Ruth Silver, the first single mother to be elected into city government.

Gordon Lau, the first Chinese American elected official in San Francisco.

Ella Hill Hutch, the first African American elected official in that same city.

Harvey understood that when one group is oppressed, no one is safe from oppression. Until everyone is free to be themselves, no one is free. He stood together with those leaders to announce that in their resistance, they were united.

Harvey had a lot of fun that first year in office. He became known as an effective lawmaker who also loved to pull pranks. Having fun and doing good, that was the Harvey Milk way.

#RESIST LESSON

OPPRESSION ISOLATES US.
RESISTANCE UNITES US.

WANGARI MAATHAI

#resist 1977

"IT'S THE LITTLE THINGS CITIZENS DO. THAT'S WHAT WILL MAKE THE DIFFERENCE. MY LITTLE THING IS PLANTING TREES."

THIS IS THE THING ABOUT planting seeds. You can water them; you can tend to them. But you never truly control how and when and if they grow. You plant the seed. You do your part. You hope for the best.

In Kenya, there was a great leader named Tom Mboya. As Kenya came to the end of its colonial era (meaning it had long been ruled by an outside government) and became independent, Mboya wanted to do something to help educate a generation of students to be leaders.

Together with Senator John F. Kennedy and Martin Luther King Jr., he devised a plan for Kenyan students to study in the

United States. Those students would be the seeds of leadership for Kenya.

Wangari Maathai was one of those seeds. Through Mboya's program, she got a scholarship to study biology at Benedictine College in Kansas. But she didn't stop there. She went on to get her master's in biology from the University of Pittsburgh. It was a great honor, but Wangari hadn't stopped learning, wouldn't stop growing. She became the first East African woman to receive her PhD. She had started as a seed, but she had grown into something far mightier.

In 1977, Wangari turned her keen mind toward helping the women in Kenya who were victims of Kenya's turbulent political system—and protecting the natural resources of her homeland, which were being exploited by greedy, powerful interests. She planted seven trees. She saw it all so clearly—how she could tie the needs of the women, who needed work, with the protection and restoration of the land. Those seven trees were the beginning of what became known as the Green Belt Movement, a program that creates jobs, combats deforestation and soil erosion, and restores a valued fuel source for cooking and generating income.

The powerful fought her, but Wangari's trees, and thousands more, grew. In 2004, she became the first African woman to win the Nobel Peace Prize. Since she began, more than fifty-one million trees have been planted and more than thirty thousand women have been trained in fields including forestry, food processing, and beekeeping.

It all started with one seed.

#RESIST LESSON

IN FORESTRY, AS IN LIFE, THERE ARE TOO MANY PEOPLE CUTTING AND NOT ENOUGH PEOPLE PLANTING.

ARCHBISHOP ÓSCAR ROMERO

#resist 1980

※

"LIKE A VOICE CRYING IN THE DESERT, WE MUST CONTINUALLY SAY 'NO' TO VIOLENCE AND 'YES' TO PEACE."

HE WANTED ONLY TO DO the work. For twenty years, Óscar Romero worked as a parish priest in the Catholic church, dedicated to helping people in his community. When he was made a bishop in 1970, he did not want to speak out against the government. He did not want to become political. It was a time when human rights abuses and a right-wing military government ruled his country, El Salvador, with violence and terror. Óscar was afraid.

Then his good friend, a Jesuit priest named Rutilio Grande,

was murdered for his work with the poor. The murder had a strange effect on Óscar. It didn't make him more afraid. Losing his friend made him *unafraid*.

He came to believe that a life lived in silence was more dangerous than one in which you spoke out for the good of the people. He began preaching a different kind of gospel—one focused on the immorality of oppression and the innate holiness of the oppressed. It was called liberation theology.

The violent regime in El Salvador didn't like this parish priest telling his downtrodden congregation to rise up—that they were divine and that their leaders were corrupt.

But Óscar didn't stop. He wasn't satisfied with merely preaching these things from the altar.

He started a radio program.

He published a newspaper.

He did not whisper the names of those who had been murdered and tortured.

He blared them across the sound waves and the front pages of his paper.

He refused to be silenced.

And in his refusal, he found a courage he never imagined he might have. Because he spoke out, the communities around him grew closer. They grew more courageous and more committed to helping each other survive the atrocities of the military government.

He said, "Let us not tire of preaching love; it is the force that will overcome the world. . . . Though we see the waves of violence succeed . . . love must win out; it is the only thing that can."

#RESIST LESSON

OUR SILENCE DOES NOT PROTECT US.

MALALA YOUSAFZAI
#resist 2009

"WHEN THE WHOLE WORLD IS SILENT, EVEN ONE VOICE BECOMES POWERFUL."

WHEN MALALA WAS TEN, THE Taliban—a hard-line, fundamentalist group—came to her village in Pakistan and forced the school that her father had founded to close. Her father was determined that she would have the same opportunity for an education that her parents did.

The Taliban saw things differently.

They banned girls from attending school. Activities such as dancing and watching television were outlawed. In the end, the Taliban closed four hundred schools.

With her father's encouragement, Malala began to stand up to the Taliban.

As with Ida B. Wells before her, journalism became her microphone.

"How dare the Taliban take away my basic right to education?" she once said on Pakistani TV.

It was a dangerous thing to say of a group that ruled by guns and force. It was a brave thing for a girl to say to men who did not believe girls had the right to go to school. Malala learned to live with two sensations in her heart: the courage to speak out, fear of what the consequences of her actions might be.

She started to blog anonymously on the Urdu-language site of the British Broadcasting Corporation (BBC). Urdu is Malala's native language.

She wrote about life in the Swat Valley under Taliban rule and about her desire to go to school. She used a pseudonym to protect herself and her family—"Gul Makai," which means "Cornflower" in Urdu.

She was eleven when she wrote her first blog post. She typed the words as plainly as she could. She wrote, "I am afraid." But even as she shared her fears, she grew in strength.

She was nominated for an International Children's Peace Prize in 2011. Later that year, she was awarded Pakistan's National Youth Peace Prize.

Then on October 9, 2012, when she was fifteen, Malala was shot by the Taliban.

The schools had reopened, thanks in part to her shining a spotlight on her oppression, and she was seated on the bus, on her way home. Two members of the Taliban stopped the bus. One of them asked for Malala by name and fired three shots at her.

One of the bullets entered her head, exited, and lodged in her shoulder. She was in grave danger and was airlifted to a Pakistani military hospital, then four days later to a hospital in Birmingham, England.

In England, Malala was taken out of a medically induced coma. She needed multiple surgeries. The left side of her face was paralyzed, and doctors needed to repair a facial nerve in hopes of fixing it. But she suffered no major brain damage. Six months after the shooting, she was able to start school in the United Kingdom.

From that moment on, it seemed that the whole world knew her story.

On her sixteenth birthday, she traveled to New York and spoke at the United Nations. In the time following her speech, her friend Shiza Shahid helped her channel all the support that was being directed toward her into a movement to educate girls all around the world. The nonprofit they founded focuses on ensuring girls twelve years of education in places where that is the most challenging—countries such as Pakistan, Afghanistan, India, Nigeria, and those housing Syrian refugees, among others.

In October 2014, she and Indian children's rights activist Kailash Satyarthi were awarded the Nobel Peace Prize. At seventeen, Malala was the youngest recipient of the award.

In her speech, Malala reminded the audience, "This award is not just for me. It is for those forgotten children who want education. It is for those frightened children who want peace. It is for those voiceless children who want change."

#RESIST LESSON

YOU ARE NOT TOO YOUNG.

JANET MOCK
#resist 2011

"A MOVEMENT IS SO MUCH MORE THAN A MARCH. A MOVEMENT IS THAT DIFFICULT SPACE BETWEEN OUR REALITY AND OUR VISION. OUR LIBERATION DEPENDS ON ALL OF US."

SHE NEVER FELT AT HOME in the body she was born in. When she was eighteen, she traveled to Bangkok to have what was then called gender reassignment surgery. She said, "I was born in what doctors proclaim is a boy's body. I had no choice in the assignment of my sex at birth. . . . Surgery did not make me a girl. I was always a girl."

A study at the UCLA School of Law estimates that there are more than 150,000 children in the United States between the ages of thirteen and seventeen who identify as transgender.

There are also an estimated 1.4 million adults who identify as transgender.

Yet despite the numbers, the work for equal rights for lesbian, gay, bisexual, and especially transgender people is still just beginning.

The transgender community faces a large amount of ignorance and fear. Many outside it simply don't understand people like Janet, and what people don't understand, they fear. When people are afraid, they look to exert control over the things they fear.

Reports show that transgender kids experience higher rates of bullying and harassment. Sometimes they are bullied by teachers and school staff—the same people who should be protecting them.

Janet Mock was living her life as a woman. She had not told very many people that she was transgender. She wasn't *hiding* it. But she didn't think it was important for people to know. Then she started reading stories about LGBT kids who were committing suicide because of the secrets they felt forced to keep. Janet knew then she had to speak out.

She made a video about her experience as a transgender woman. She spoke about having what is now called "gender affirmation surgery." She became a television correspondent and an antibullying activist. She created a Twitter hashtag called #girlslikeus.

In speaking out, she saved lives. She inspired and educated millions of Americans. Audre Lorde, the black, lesbian, activist poet, once wrote, "And at last you'll know with surpassing certainty that only one thing is more frightening than speaking your truth. And that is not speaking." Janet Mock refuses to live in fear.

#RESIST LESSON

FREEDOM MUST BE INCLUSIVE.

REV. DR. WILLIAM J. BARBER II

#resist 2013

꙳

"WE MUST SHOCK THIS NATION WITH THE POWER OF LOVE. WE MUST SHOCK THIS NATION WITH THE POWER OF MERCY. WE MUST SHOCK THIS NATION AND FIGHT FOR JUSTICE FOR ALL. WE CAN'T GIVE UP ON THE HEART OF OUR DEMOCRACY, NOT NOW, NOT EVER!"

HE KNEW THE IMPORTANCE OF voting rights.

The Reverend William Barber, pastor of the Greenleaf Christian Church in Goldsboro, North Carolina, had studied the work of Frederick Douglass and Susan B. Anthony, Fannie

Lou Hamer, Martin Luther King Jr., and John Lewis before him.

So in 2012, when members of the Republican Party in North Carolina began an all-out attack on voting rights, he knew that there could be no hesitancy in fighting back.

The right to vote is too precious.

The battles had been too hard-won.

Political differences were to be expected, even encouraged, in a democracy.

But voting rights were sacred.

He said, "Wait a minute. This has gone too far."

One Monday, he led a small group of religious leaders and activists to the state legislative building in Raleigh. They sang "We Shall Overcome," a beloved song from the civil rights era. They read from the Bible and then stood in front of the senate chambers. The police led them away in handcuffs.

The following Monday, more than a hundred people joined them. Then thousands came. Some weeks a crowd of eighty thousand gathered to stand with Reverend Barber. It was a simple idea that turned the first day of the workweek into a day when people gathered to do the work of resistance: Moral Mondays.

Morality is a tricky word. What one person considers right another person might consider wrong. But Reverend Barber and the people who stood with him believed that there are some things that almost every American can agree are right, that these are the morals of the modern age that must guide us.

He said, "Some issues are not left or right or liberal versus conservative. They are right versus wrong."

The people who gathered on Moral Mondays were united in their belief that every American deserves the right to vote—without undue requirements or random restrictions, aimed at keeping poor and minority voters away from the polls. They also believed every citizen is entitled to affordable health care. Reverend Barber said, "The fight for health care is the fight for the soul of America."

The people of Moral Mondays revived Dr. Martin Luther King Jr.'s Poor People's Campaign and have taken it to the most vulnerable communities across America. They feed the poor. They let them know that they are not alone.

Reverend Barber reminds us that when we come together to make a difference, when we put the needs of others ahead of our own, when we lead with our hearts, we can make a difference. We can knock down walls. He said, "It is our turn now to change the country. The first victory is when we decide to fight together."

#RESIST LESSON

WE CAN'T TAKE FOR GRANTED THE RIGHTS WE CHERISH. THEY NEED CONTINUAL PROTECTING.

ALICIA GARZA, PATRISSE CULLORS, AND OPAL TOMETI

#BLACKLIVESMATTER

#resist 2013

> "OF COURSE, ALL LIVES MATTER. BUT #ALLLIVESMATTER EFFECTIVELY NEUTRALIZES THE FACT THAT IT'S BLACK PEOPLE WHO ARE FIGHTING FOR THEIR LIVES RIGHT NOW."
>
> —Alicia Garza

WHEN THE VERDICT CAME IN on the shooting death of an unarmed teenager named Trayvon Martin, Alicia was sitting in a bar with her husband and friends. After sixteen hours of deliberation, the jury had returned what felt like a lynching-era verdict. A white man had been found not guilty in what appeared to be a racially motivated crime.

The room fell silent, and Alicia said, "The one thing I remember from that evening, other than crying myself to sleep that night, was the way in which as a black person, I felt incredibly vulnerable, incredibly exposed, and incredibly enraged. Seeing these black people leaving the bar, and it was like we couldn't look at each other. We were carrying this burden around with us every day: of racism and white supremacy. It was a verdict that said: Black people are not safe in America."

The struggle for her was also personal. Young Trayvon Martin reminded her of boys she knew and loved. "My brother is six feet tall and has a huge Afro," Alicia said, "and I thought, That could have been my family."

That night, she logged on to Facebook and wrote what she called "essentially a love note to black people" and posted it on her page. The last line read: "Black people. I love you. I love us. Our lives matter."

Patrisse, a close friend, read Alicia's post in a hotel three hundred miles away. Patrisse, who works in prison reform and as a community organizer, began sharing Alicia's words online. She added the hashtag #blacklivesmatter.

The next day, Patrisse and Alicia reached out to a third friend, Opal, who worked in immigrant rights. They strategized about how to share the hashtag across social media but also about how to take it offline into real-life protests. "We wanted to connect people who were already buzzing about all this stuff and get them to do something, not just retweet or like or share," Alicia said. "We thought, How do we get folks together and take that energy and create something awesome?"

Black Lives Matter now has forty-two chapters, each with its own localized mission and work.

In Chicago, the group helped bring about the firing of a police superintendent when they learned that he had withheld footage of the shooting of an unarmed teenager for more than a year.

In Baton Rouge, in the wake of the police shooting of Alton Sterling, the activists filed—and won—a lawsuit stating the city's militarized police were overly aggressive and used "unconstitutional tactics" against protesters.

In California, students and activists protested until the University of California withdrew $30 million that the school had, amid much controversy, invested in private prisons.

Congresswoman Barbara Lee of California called the Black Lives Matter movement a necessary check and balance to the powers that be. "They've brought the necessary 'street heat' to drive change and hold elected officials accountable. This movement, largely driven by young people, is really the civil and human rights struggle of our time."

The movement has inspired actors, artists, and athletes. In 2016, Beyoncé's Super Bowl halftime show brought the Black Lives Matter movement alive with music and dance. Tennis legend Serena Williams wrote an essay in *Wired* magazine: "To those of you involved in equality movements like Black Lives Matter, I say this: Keep it up." At the ESPY Awards that same year, basketball greats LeBron James, Carmelo Anthony, Dwyane Wade, and Chris Paul cited the movement and called for an end to racial violence.

The movement has encountered critics who see it as a kind of reverse racism: #alllivesmatter became a popular and controversial hashtag. In July 2016, a few days after the shooting of Alton Sterling, President Barack Obama defended the naming of the movement when he said, "When people say 'black lives matter,' it doesn't mean 'blue lives' don't matter, it just means all lives matter." Obama went on to say, "But right now the big concern is the fact that the data shows black folks are more vulnerable to these kinds of incidents. . . . To be concerned about these issues is not political correctness. It's just being American and wanting to live up to our best and highest ideals."

A young woman sat alone in her room and wrote an impassioned Facebook post. Her friends were reading, listening, and together they decided to carry the weight of their heartache toward the goalposts of activism and change.

Just like that, a movement was born.

#RESIST LESSON

INJUSTICE NEED NOT RENDER YOU POWERLESS.

ANASTASIA SOMOZA

#resist 2016

🌿

"I'M STRIVING TO PIONEER A NEW NORMAL, WITH AND FOR INDIVIDUALS WITH DISABILITIES."

WHEN SHE WAS NINE YEARS old, Anastasia Somoza got an incredible opportunity. She was invited to visit the White House and meet the president. What would you do with that opportunity? What would you ask the president of the United States?

For Anastasia, the question she wanted to ask was very clear.

Anastasia and her twin sister, Alba, were both born prematurely, with cerebral palsy and spastic quadriplegia.

Anastasia was verbal and was able to move quickly into mainstream classes. Alba, who could not talk, was shuffled into special-ed classes and denied the education she deserved.

Anastasia asked President Bill Clinton to help her get her sister into mainstream classes.

Two years after Anastasia's White House visit, and as the result of the tireless work of her and her parents, Anastasia achieved their goal.

Alba, who used computers to speak, was placed in a regular class. It was the beginning of what Anastasia called "our inclusion revolution." Anastasia became a tireless advocate for disabled people from that point forward. She pushed herself to achieve all that she could so that others could look at her and see not her disability, but her profound talents and *abilities*.

Anastasia went on to study at Georgetown University and the London School of Economics. Being quadriplegic did not lower her bar for what is possible. She worked with the Clinton Foundation on an initiative to end the abandonment of babies with disabilities in China. She scaled the Great Wall of China, both literally and figuratively.

Anastasia's sister thrived, too. Former President Clinton attended her high school graduation. Through a groundbreaking therapy program, her communication skills improved dramatically. Alba studied at Queens College and the Met, New York's famed Metropolitan Museum of Art.

Alba is now a visual artist, gives tours at the Met, and teaches art to kids of all levels of ability.

For both sisters, the mission is clear: close the ignorance gap around people with disabilities, and the realm of what is possible is thrown wide open.

#RESIST LESSON

THE WORLD MAY LOOK AT YOU AND SAY, "YOU CAN'T." YOU MUST KNOW IN YOUR HEART THAT YOU CAN.

THE MILLION WOMEN OF THE WOMEN'S MARCH

#resist 2017

"MAKE SURE YOU INTRODUCE YOURSELVES TO EACH OTHER AND DECIDE WHAT WE'RE GOING TO DO TOMORROW AND TOMORROW AND TOMORROW AND WE'RE NEVER TURNING BACK."

—Gloria Steinem

THEY WOKE BEFORE SUNRISE ON a cold January morning.

They carried signs and cups of coffee in their hands.

They carried hope and a quest for justice in their hearts.

The signs read:

"A WOMAN'S PLACE IS IN THE RESISTANCE."

"GRAB 'EM BY THE PATRIARCHY."

"MAKE AMERICA THINK AGAIN."

"FEMINISM IS THE RADICAL NOTION THAT WOMEN ARE *PEOPLE*."

Many of them wore pink hats with cat ears, a sly reference to offensive remarks made by President Donald Trump that were uncovered during his campaign.

What the cameras showed was a sea of faces: every color, every age, wearing pink knitted hats: a stunning display of woman power.

It began as a single post. On November 9, 2016, the day after the surprising election of Donald Trump as president of the United States, Teresa Shook, a grandmother from Maui, Hawaii, created a Facebook page and invited her friends to march on Washington.

The march was set for the weekend of the inauguration of Donald Trump, a man who many citizens did not feel was fit to be president of the United States. To mark their protest, to let those in government know that the people would be watching and demanding that their rights be protected, millions of American women, their partners, their children, their families, their allies, and their friends, decided to march.

Other Facebook pages, by people such as Bob Bland, Evie Harmon, Fontaine Pearson, and Breanne Butler, appeared around the same time. Bland, Harmon, Pearson, and Butler decided to unite their efforts alongside Carmen Perez, Tamika Mallory, and Linda Sarsour.

Nobody knew how many people would come out to march. All they knew was that marching was the legacy of the strong and the purposeful.

In 1913, Inez Milholland donned a cape, mounted a horse, and led a crowd of five thousand women down the streets of Washington, DC, in support of the Nineteenth Amendment, which would give women the right to vote. President William Howard Taft took side streets to a hotel to avoid the marchers. Others mocked and attacked the women. *The New York Times* reported that one police officer threatened a woman, saying, "If my wife were where you are, I'd break her head."

In 1930, in protest of the British salt tax, Mohandas Gandhi organized a march from his ashram (a place of Hindu worship) to the Arabian Sea to collect salt. The crowds gathered on the journey, and more than sixty thousand Indian citizens were arrested. The salt march would give Gandhi greater bargaining power with the British and inspire future leaders around the world.

Dr. Martin Luther King Jr. had marched on Washington for civil rights. On August 28, 1963, more than a quarter-million people gathered in Washington to stand with him.

In 1969, more than half a million Americans marched on Washington again, calling for the end of the Vietnam War. That war had killed more young people than any in modern history: 242 young Americans died in just one seven-day period.

In 1981, when air traffic controllers went on strike, calling for better pay and safer working conditions, 260,000 Americans flocked to Washington, DC, for a "Solidarity March."

The next year, in 1982, a million protesters flooded New York's Central Park in a march protesting the use of nuclear weapons.

In 1993, more than eight hundred thousand protesters marched for the support of lesbian, gay, and bisexual equal rights. Together, they demanded a bill against discrimination and increased funding for AIDS research.

In 1995, African American leaders gathered a million supporters in Washington for the historic Million Man March.

In 2004, 1.1 million pro-choice activists gathered in Washington for the March for Women's Lives.

But what happened in 2017 was unlike anything the world had ever seen. Five million protesters in over five hundred cities and towns around the world marched.

What was so striking was the number of locations. People were marching wherever they were—a powerful reminder that you can #resist wherever you are.

There were ten thousand protesters in Detroit, Michigan, and another ten thousand in Pocatello, Idaho. In Antarctica, more than one hundred passengers organized and gathered on a ship.

Four hundred and eight of the marches took place in the United States, and another 168 marches happened in eighty-one countries around the world.

In Boston, Massachusetts, Senator Elizabeth Warren told the crowds in her home state that "we can whimper, we can whine, or we can fight back. Me, I'm here to fight back."

It was the largest organized protest in US history.

One of the largest in the world.

It was a call to protect not just women's rights, but human rights. To uplift not just the people, but the planet.

The president had begun, even before he was elected, to threaten the rights of immigrants, ignoring the fact that America, more than almost any nation on earth, is a country of immigrants. He threatened to build a wall to keep out those seeking a better life in America. The protesters stood in unity, promising to tear down any such wall.

As the president had repeatedly denied the importance of climate change, the women's marchers went on record that they wanted to make the Earth safe not only for themselves, but for generations to come.

It was a reminder that a march is one of the most powerful tools at our disposal in a democracy. Marches remind leaders that the power of the people is always greater than the people in power.

At the march in Washington, Congressman John Lewis

encouraged the crowds to "bend toward justice. I'm ready to march again. I've come here to say to you: Don't let anybody, anybody, turn you around."

#RESIST LESSON

ALWAYS BE READY TO MARCH AGAIN.

Joan of Arc Martin Luther Bull Chiune Ma

Samuel Adams Sojourner Sugiha

Ozen the Apache Warrior Truth Osk

Susan B. Anthony Gandhi Schin

ween Liliuokalani Mar

miliano Zapata Ida B. Wells Luth

Lucretia Mott King

Dietrich Bonhoeffer Malcolm

Hedy Lamarr X La

Dolores Cesar Chavez Miriam

nnie Lou Hamer Makeba

arvey Milk Rachel Carson

angari Maathai Archbishop

jari Oscar Rom

Janet Mock opal ti Malala Yousaf

❧ AFTERWORD ❧

MY EDITOR AND I WERE nearly finished with this project when news broke of a shooting at Marjory Stoneman Douglas High School in Parkland, Florida. Seventeen students and educators were killed in the attack.

The classmates of those who died, the survivors of the attack, knew that what had happened in their school, and in countless communities across the country, was wrong. They knew too many students had become victims of gun violence, and they decided to take a stand. "The Parkland Kids," as they have been called, launched a national movement and just weeks after a terrible tragedy organized the March for Our Lives—the largest single-day protest ever held in our nation's capital. (You can find out more about their ongoing efforts at www.marchforourlives.com.)

This is eerily fitting—since the woman for whom the school in Parkland was named was also a resister. Marjory Stoneman Douglas was a journalist at a time when very few women were allowed to work as reporters. She agitated for women's right to vote and for the protection of the Florida Everglades.

But resistance goes on. It's not past. It is our present, our every day.

Resistance is not only the realm of adults. As we see now, and within our recent history, young people have consistently been this country's greatest motivators for change. The Parkland Kids are no exception.

We are honored to present the words of Samantha Fuentes, one of Parkland's survivors and a recipient of the 2018 PEN Freedom of Expression Courage award.

Sam's recollections and her words are raw and may be disturbing to some readers. They are at the same time an inspiration to continue to resist, even when faced with the greatest odds, against injustice.

—*Veronica Chambers*

HELLO, MY NAME IS SAMANTHA Fuentes, and on February 14, 2018, my life was changed forever when I was shot in my classroom at Marjory Stoneman Douglas High School. I suffered a gunshot wound in my left leg, and pieces of shrapnel were embedded within my face, behind my eyeball, and in various other locations in my legs. It took multiple surgeries, time, therapy, and tears to rebuild. Healing hurts, but it's not impossible.

As human beings, we're quite strange. We train, restrain, practice, and revise, spending so much time making ourselves uncomfortable in order to be comfortable. We hide ourselves and our impulses, trying to fit into labels and dress sizes, because society tells us if we don't meet some unspoken standard, we are not worthy. We'll be left behind if we don't make at least a bare minimum, so we strive for the things that make our moms and mentors satisfied. Achieving gold-star status, but left with a last-place feeling inside.

Being just enough never is. Ever since February 14 I've met people who cry when they've just met me. They've sent their stuffed animals, thoughts, prayers, and kindness. They've told me to rest, to heal, to grieve; they've told me I've been through enough and I don't have to fight anymore. At first I didn't want to fight—I didn't have strength or courage. Then I grew restless, angry, and disappointed. It seemed the world had instantly ignored my cries, justice was not being served, I was not satisfied, but I was scared to act, to speak. . . . But then I opened my eyes and shifted my focus to kids just like me instead of to the leaders who ignored me.

My strength was found the in strangest of places. Sometimes it was in a letter by an elementary school kid from Texas, or school walkouts in Colorado, or bumper stickers on cars, or your traumatized friends speaking in front of hundreds only days after the tragedy. At first it was only a twinkle in a very gloomy, dark world. The more I chased that dim twinkle, the more it started to shine like the sun. I achieved strength through hope. Through listening to the words of support and encouragement, and believing them for myself.

I wanted to be that twinkle, so bad. I wanted to be the mentors I lost. I wanted to be that beacon of hope my peers provided for me. I wanted to be the friend for those who lost theirs. I wanted to be a voice of reason in the sea of disarray and background noise. More than anything, I didn't want a single child to worry about being killed or injured, anywhere. I didn't want a single child to be like me.

Resilience is the key to making a difference in the world

around you, because making a difference might mean taking risks, speaking the truth out loud, saying no to those you must obey, and overcoming obstacles you've never faced. The ability to point out flaws in a system that believes that YOU are the flaw. That's true resilience. That's true strength.

It isn't something to be feared or feel excluded from: Everyone can be strong, everyone can make a difference in some way. The question is how. Embrace strength, because the kind that I found,

I found it in my weakest moments.

Joan of Arc
Martin Luther Sojourner Chiune Ma
Samuel Adams Truth Sugiha
Ozen the Apache Warrior Schin
Susan B. Anthony Gandhi Mar
ween Liliuokalani Luth
miliano Zapata Ida B. Wells King
Lucretia Mott
Dietrich Bonhoeffer Malcolm
Hedy Lamarr Malcolm X La
Dolores Cesar Chavez
nnie Lou Huerta Miriam
Harvey Hamer Makeba
angari Milk Rachel Carson
ari Maathai Archbishop
Oscar Ro
Mark Opal Malala Yousaf

LEARN MORE ABOuT THE POWER OF RESISTANCE

READ:

Who Was Joan of Arc?, by Pam Pollack and Meg Belviso

Joan of Arc, by Josephine Poole

Renegade: Martin Luther, the Graphic Biography, by Dacia Palmerino and Andrea Ciponte

Along Came Galileo, by Jeanne Bendick

Frederick Douglass: The Lion Who Wrote History, by Walter Dean Myers

Sitting Bull: Lakota Warrior and Defender of His People, by S. D. Nelson

The Gift of Anger: And Other Lessons from My Grandfather Mahatma Gandhi, by Arun Gandhi

Emiliano Zapata!: Revolution and Betrayal in Mexico, by Samuel Brunk

Bonhoeffer: Pastor, Martyr, Prophet, Spy, Student Edition, by Eric Metaxas

Hedy Lamarr and a Secret Communication System, a graphic novel by Trina Robbins, Cynthia Martin, and Anne Timmons

The Sense of Wonder: A Celebration of Nature for Parents and Children, by Rachel Carson

Unbowed: A Memoir, by Wangari Maathai

The Violence of Love, by Óscar Romero

When They Call You a Terrorist: A Black Lives Matter Memoir, by Patrisse Khan-Cullors and asha bandele

WATCH:

Joan of Arc, by Victor Fleming, starring Ingrid Bergman as Joan, a classic film that won two Academy Awards

Torchlighters, "The Martin Luther Story," starring Stephen Daltry

Nova, "Galileo's Battle for the Heavens"

Life of Sojourner Truth: Ain't I a Woman?, a *Booklist* Selected Video for Young Adults

American Lives: "Not for Ourselves Alone: The Story of Elizabeth Cady Stanton & Susan B. Anthony," by Ken Burns

Sugihara: Conspiracy of Kindness, by Robert Kirk

Schindler's List, by Steven Spielberg

Road to Peace: Ancient Wisdom of the 14th Dalai Lama of Tibet, a documentary about the Dalai Lama, by Leon Stuparich

Dolores, by Peter Bratt

Selma, by acclaimed director Ava DuVernay

Malcolm X, by Spike Lee

The Times of Harvey Milk, by Robert Epstein

He Named Me Malala, an inspiring documentary about the life of Malala Yousafzai, by Davis Guggenheim

The Trans List, a documentary about notable transgender people, by Timothy Greenfield-Sanders

LISTEN:

Frederick Douglass: Stuff You Missed in History Class, podcast by How Stuff Works

Every Tone a Testimony: An African American Aural History, from the collection of Smithsonian Folkway Recordings. This recording features "Speech at Akron Convention," by Sojourner Truth; "What to the Slave Is the Fourth of July?," by Frederick Douglass;

"Lynching Our National Crime," by Ida B. Wells; an interview with Angela Davis; and the Student Nonviolent Coordinating Committee Freedom Singers singing "Ain't Gonna Let Nobody Turn Me Around."

Long Walk to Freedom: The Autobiography of Nelson Mandela, audiobook

Martin Luther King, Jr.: The Essential Box Set: The Landmark Speeches and Sermons of Martin Luther King Jr.

An Evening with Belafonte/Makeba, by Harry Belafonte and Miriam Makeba

Joan of Arc Martin Luther Chiune Sugihara
Samuel Adams Sojourner Truth Osk
Ozen the Apache Warrior Schin
Susan B. Anthony Gandhi Ma
ween Queen Liliuokalani Luth
miliano Zapata Ida B. Wells King
Lucretia Mott
Dietrich Bonhoeffer Malcolm
Hedy Lamarr X La
Dolores Cesar Chavez
Huerta Miriam Makeba
annie Lou Hamer
Harvey Milk Rachel Carso
angari Maathai Archbishop
ari Oscar Ro
Opal Malala Yous

ACKNOWLEDGMENTS

AS A KID WHEN I learned about historical heroes, I always imagined that they were fearless. And as someone who had a great many fears, I demoted myself to the rank of nonhero almost immediately and without thought. Writing this book, connecting the dots between contemporary figures such as Malala Yousafzai and Janet Mock and historical figures like Harvey Milk, Fannie Lou Hamer, and Dolores Huerta, I realized how important it is that we teach children (and adults) that courage is rarely a full-on display of charging into battle, like in the movies. We step up, we sit in, we march, and sometimes we take a step back, retreat, refill, rethink, and step up again.

Thank you to Senator Cory Booker for your work and for being such an inspiration. You remind us all that the power of the people is greater than the people in power. I am so grateful for your introduction to this book and for your amazing team, including Matt Klapper, Jeff Giertz, and Adam Topper.

I'm very thankful to Kristen Pettit for having the idea for

this book and for being such a powerful #resist activist both on and off the page. My literary agent, Kimberly Witherspoon, is a fierce woman warrior. I'm lucky to work with her and the Inkwell team, including Jessica Mileo.

Huge thanks to everyone at HarperCollins, but especially Elizabeth Lynch, Renée Cafiero, and Bethany Reis.

A few friends were great resources and readers for me on this book: Thank you, Hitha Palepu, Rachel Bowie, and Samantha Shankman.

A personal thank-you to my home team: Jason Clampet; Flora Clampet; my parents, Cecilia and Antonio Ortega; and my in-laws, Jerry and Mary Clampet.

My deepest appreciation to Wendy Zipes Hunter for connecting us with the #NeverAgain movement. I'm so thankful to Samantha Fuentes for adding her voice to this story, and to her mother, Carmen Cruz, for being a light.

Bard College at Simon's Rock is where my own activism began to grow. I'm very grateful to that community, including Pat Sharpe, Arthur and Louise Hillman, Jim Monson, Bernie Rodgers, Ian Bickford, and Emily H. Fisher.

The gift of being alive and living in a democracy—even one that is flawed—is that we have a voice. We choose, every day, whether or not to use it. As Alice Walker so memorably put it, "The most common way people give up their power is by thinking they don't have any." I hope this book is a reminder of the power and potential in us all.